THE LONG SUMMER

45 COMMANDO RM 1963–1964

ADEN, TANGANYIKA AND THE RADFAN

BY

LT COL T M P 'PADDY' STEVENS
OBE MC RM

SERIES EDITOR
CAPTAIN DEREK OAKLEY MBE RM

ROYAL MARINES HISTORICAL SOCIETY
SPECIAL PUBLICATION NO 35

THE LONG SUMMER: 45 COMMANDO RM 1963–1964

ISBN 978 0 9536163 6 7

First published 2009 by the
ROYAL MARINES HISTORICAL SOCIETY
Royal Marines Museum
Eastney
Southsea
Hants PO4 9PX
United Kingdom

Printed and bound in Great Britain by
CPI Antony Rowe, Chippenham and Eastbourne

Acknowledgements

The Royal Marines Historical Society is most indebted to Mrs Judy Stevens for allowing us to publish her husband's memoirs of his time as the Commanding Officer of 45 Commando Royal Marines. His tour in Aden from July 1963 to November 1964 covered not only exercises and unrest in Aden, but also the sudden unit deployment to Tanganyika and later, service in the rugged up country 'war' against the rebels in the Radfan. This is one of the few personal accounts by a Commando CO on active service. It was brought to our attention by his daughter Mandy, who found the manuscript 'literally in the attic' and also former Royal Marines officer James Barr. There is a copy of the original in the Royal Marines Museum archives.

The text used is exactly as Lt Col 'Paddy' Stevens wrote it and the majority of the photographs are his. We have added maps and a few extra photographs, which have come from a number of sources including Ted Goddard and James Barr. The maps are from David Young's book *Four Five: the History of 45 Commando* published by Leo Cooper Ltd in 1972.

'Paddy' Stevens joined the Royal Marines in January 1940 and was serving as a Troop Commander with 41 (RM) Commando when he was decorated with the Military Cross for gallant and distinguished services during the landings in Normandy, later being presented with it in the field by General Sir Bernard Montgomery. He was subsequently awarded the OBE for his services with 45 Commando RM that he describes in this book.

'Radfan Paddy'

Contents

Glossary of Maps

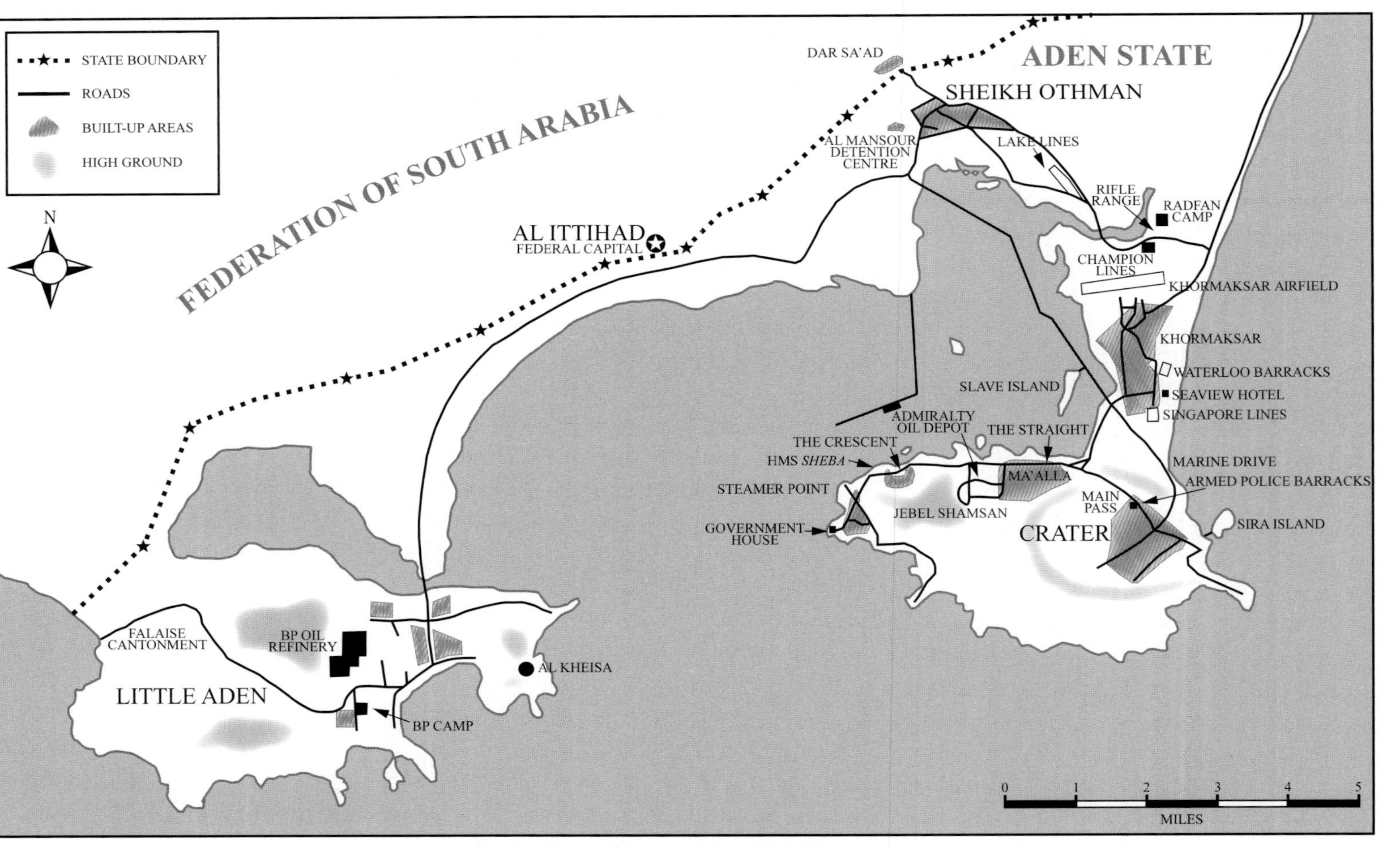

Internal Security, Aden 1964–67

Preface

From time to time some part of the Armed Forces hits the headlines. There is a crisis overseas, and a unit is flown from England or launched into an operation from a British base. There may even be fighting. Newspaper correspondents arrive, and the papers carry vivid accounts of the operations, and sometimes the personal stories of the men taking part. Then the crisis is past, and the newspapers are filled with other and more important matters. The units that have taken part in the operations disappear from the eyes of the public and are not heard of again for many years, if at all.

In between these times the ships and battalions and air squadrons are still spread out over the world, going about their business more or less quietly, waiting in the wings for their next cue, or for one of many different cues – codewords, that will call them out to play any one of a number of different parts. Sometimes they are relaxing. Most of the time they are rehearsing some of their parts, and trying to guess what the next cue will be and when it will come.

This is a story of peace-time soldiering in one unit: 45 Commando, Royal Marines, from the middle of 1963 until late 1964. We had our brief moments of fame, during the Tanganyika crisis and in the early stages of the Radfan campaign. In fact 1964 seemed to us a very busy year by any standards, and there were few days when there were not some men of the unit with live ammunition in their rifles watching their front very closely indeed.

Most units that have served abroad in the last twenty years could tell a similar story – of being thrown suddenly into unexpected operations, of fighting in strange landscapes, the interminable hours of waiting and watching, or of training for the unknown; and, in between, managing to enjoy themselves quietly or noisily according to taste. We did no more and no less than most. There are no great battles here, and we were lucky in having so few casualties – though there were several times when it might have been otherwise.

I have touched on the political background of the operations only in so far as it directly affected what we were doing. On the military side, I have given only passing mention to HMS *Centaur*'s work during the Tanganyika operation, and to the many other units and supporting arms, including the RAF and the naval helicopters, which fought in the Radfan. To describe everything would require a different kind of book. This is a personal account, peace-time soldiering seen through the eyes of one Commanding Officer, his life inevitably tied to that of his unit.

The presence of a Royal Marine Commando in what is mainly an Army setting requires a word of explanation. The Royal Marines are amphibious soldiers, trained to land from ships in helicopters or landing craft. Once ashore their work is mainly infantry work, and Commandos are organised and equipped much like infantry battalions. When they are not embarked they earn their keep as infantry battalions. Since World War II they have operated by land and sea in many places – Palestine, Malaya, Korea, Cyprus, Suez, Kuwait, East Africa, Southern Arabia and Borneo.

This is the story of how 45 Commando, Royal Marines, earned its keep in 1964, the year of the 300th anniversary of the formation of the Royal Marines.

Chapter 1

Aden

In 1947, bound for the Far East in a troopship, I went ashore at Aden. It was hot and dusty, and the harsh volcanic hills rising above the town gave it a depressing air. I returned on board by the first boat.

*

In 1959, as a staff officer, I visited Aden to discuss the move there of 45 Commando from Malta. I spent a week in Aden, saw nothing to change my original impression of it, and was glad to return to a place of coolness and comfort.

*

On 11 July 1963 I landed at Khormaksar Airfield, appointed to command 45 Commando. It was early morning, but a blast of heat swept into the aircraft as the door opened. Walking across the tarmac the heat seemed to come from everywhere, bouncing off the airport buildings and off the ground and suspended in the air. My predecessor was waiting for me with the adjutant. We drove the twenty miles across the causeway and the desert road to Little Aden. Within an hour, after a shower and breakfast, he began to hand over the Commando. I saw him off at Khormaksar three days later, and found myself alone and in command.

Those who serve in Aden either like it or loathe it, and I soon came to like it. It is hot, it is not beautiful, and life is bounded in many ways. Yet for those who are prepared to accept its limitations it has much to offer.

'Aden', of course, is only a part of it, the town and port with the small State of Aden around it, embracing Little Aden with its great BP oil refinery and its military camps, ten miles to the west across the harbour. This State is one of several of the Federation of South Arabia, stretching 100 miles westwards to Perim Island at the entrance to the Red Sea; northwards 100 miles or more over high mountains to the borders of Yemen; eastwards 200 miles to the Eastern Protectorate and the Hadramaut.

The term 'Aden' is often used loosely, for the town or for the State or even for the whole country we lived and worked in. I shall use it loosely, and trust that its precise meaning is obvious from the context.

Aden State and the rest of the Federation are different worlds. Aden is a modern city of 200,000 people; an elected government and trades unions, social services and modern hospitals; modern schools with smartly-dressed and lively children around them; great offices, rich houses and appalling slums; noisy Arab markets and lines of modern shops; Arabs in European dress or in colourful turbans and skirts, black-veiled women and old, blind beggars; narrow back-streets, at night full of sleeping men, and broad double carriageways with streams of modern cars sweeping noisily past.

Around, in the flat countryside, are some fertile areas where the picture is different only in degree. Beyond the plains it is a different world: high and barren mountains; small patches of cultivation surviving on erratic rainfall; small groups of thick-walled houses with tiny windows, fort-like houses, guarding the fields; few roads other than camel tracks; the thin population split up by the country into tribes and sub-tribes, fiercely independent and jealous; tough hillmen, very proud, bound by tradition and custom, often poor, often diseased – a feudal world, where the Rulers have little direct control over their territories, a world of quarrels over land and cattle and sometimes over women, of blood-feuds, settled, if at all, with the rifle.

Once, many centuries ago, there were elaborate systems of dams and irrigation channels in the mountains, to store and spread the erratic flood-waters. Generations of anarchy and tribal wars and blood-feuds have destroyed it all.

Aden State itself is full of conflicts and contradictions. It has grown astonishingly within this century, and strangers have poured in with the chance of work in the town and port. Nearly half the population are believed to be Yemeni subjects – it is a floating population, the families often returning home after making their small pile. Many of the rest are Arabs from other parts of the Federation, and Somalis, Indians and Pakistanis. There is disagreement about who, in fact, are Adeni, and therefore have a right to vote; there are conflicts between the groups; there are powerful and vocal trades unions; there is the fear the town Arabs have of the warlike tribes in the hills, and a reluctance to dissipate the city's wealth over the vast Federation.

And there are the British.

Like many other places, Aden fell into British hands almost by accident in the 19th century. A ship was plundered there, a British warship arrived, and in 1839 Aden was signed over to the British in exchange for annual payments to the Sultan of Lahej. Nobody minded. Aden was a village of 500 individuals, and not much of a catch. There was a fine natural harbour, though, and later in the century, after the opening of the Suez Canal, it became an important coaling station. By 1963 it was not only an oiling station but an important base, a jumping-off place to enable Britain to meet her treaty obligations and to protect her great oil interests in the Middle East.

The country inland has never 'belonged' to the British; there was never any attempt to gain political or military control over it. Britain's main concern was preventing anyone else from dominating it and thereby threatening Aden. From time to time the Egyptians, the Turks and the Yemenis invaded or interfered in the mountains, and in due course were evicted, by the British and the tribes. From time to time the British were invited to restore law and order in some of the States. All in all the mountain tribes remained independent, and jealous of their independence.

In the late 1950s a movement grew among the Rulers to join together for political and economic progress. The Federation of South Arabia was formed, and in January 1963, Aden State joined the Federation.

The British military base at that time was complementary to the base in Kenya. It consisted of the RAF airfield at Khormaksar, with its strike and transport aircraft; an armoured car regiment and part of a tank regiment; artillery, engineers and administrative services; and two infantry units, 1st Bn King's Own Scottish Borderers and 45 Commando Royal Marines.

These troops had little to do with the Federation, which was policed by the four Arab battalions of the Federal Regular Army (FRA) and by the Federal National Guard (FNG). The gunners and the armoured car regiment had detachments up-country supporting the FRA; the RAF were called in occasionally; the Commando had a company camp at Dhala near the Yemen border, for training. Most of the time, the troops trained for the many tasks they might be called upon to do anywhere in the Middle East. The last time the base had switched to full power had been over the Kuwait crisis of 1961, when 45 Commando had been the first unit to arrive by air.

Wessex helicopters landing in Little Aden near oil refineries

The Commando lived at Little Aden. It was a twenty-mile drive from the centre of Aden around the great harbour, across a causeway, then along the fast, level desert road past the bright modern buildings of the new Federal Capital at Al Ittihad.

There was not much at Little Aden: a jagged pile of grey volcanic hills, almost sheer in places; the BP refinery with its hundreds of storage tanks, its plant, its oiling jetties, its tall tower with the red flame burning day and night; the clean village built for the Arab workers by BP, and a few shops; an Arab fishing village tucked behind the hills in one of the many bays.

The Commando camp was, at best, unattractive. Tucked between the refinery and the sea, it consisted of rows of long, low huts surrounded by loose sand. It had been built by BP ten years before as temporary accommodation for the workers building the refinery. It had since been rented from BP by the Services as a temporary camp; and because it was a temporary camp little money had been spent on it. It was habitable; the huts were air-conditioned and clean; a few essential improvements had been made, it had football pitches nearby; it was only a few minutes walk from the sea and a pleasant bathing beach.

It was not paradise.

For all this, and though it was the height of summer, and hot, I found the unit in fine form. They had been to Kenya for a month's training earlier in the year, and they had had enough to do since to keep them busy and cheerful. We had no families with us, and the men only served a year with the unit – except the commanding officer, who served eighteen months. With only a year to do they were all prepared to work hard and play hard and accept the discomforts of life in Aden.

I wandered round the unit, poking my nose into odd corners, speaking to every man I met. I was satisfied. It was an efficient unit; the men were fit, lively and cheerful, and there was a rare spirit of cohesion and loyalty – the credit side, perhaps, of having them all together in a primitive place with no distractions other than those they could find within the life of the unit.

I had not previously commanded a unit; and I was out of practice, having been away from Commandos for too long. Service on the staff is not the best preparation for command of an operational unit, where quickness of decision and singleness of purpose are infinitely more important than the balanced and reasoned arguments of the staff officer. These are qualities that only come with experience. Besides, I had certain ideas of my own on training that I wanted to try out. The Commando was obviously ready for operations now if required; but I felt I would like six months before being launched into a major operation.

I got my six months, with a few days to spare.

Chapter 2

The Testing Ground

There is a curious and fundamental problem in peace-time soldiering that is not always obvious. The farmer and factory-worker have end-products; the shop-keeper or business-man has an end-product of a kind, or at least a balance-sheet in which he can measure his success or failure. A military unit in peacetime can only be measured by its appearance. It is like a car factory that produces no cars. You can inspect the buildings, test the men at their particular skills; you can see the machinery working and the assembly belt moving, without a single car on it and with the men going through the correct motions around it: but nothing comes out at the end – until one day, at a touch on a button, this factory is expected to produce its end-product instantaneously, continuously and with perfect efficiency.

In a sense, of course, the end-product of peace-time training is the appearance of the unit – not the gloss but the appearance it gives on training and exercises and the efficiency with which it performs its peace-time duties. There are professional skills that can be measured, such as marksmanship with a rifle and technical ability with radios and vehicles; skill in movement by day and night and skill in tactics; the soundness of administration in the field. You can hold tough exercises, and often make them quite realistic. The one absolute measure, success in battle, is missing.

Always, too, there is something more missing, the elements of danger and fear and the high risks of war. Always, even in the best of peacetime training, there is unreality. You are eternally preparing for something you hope will never happen.

'...you hope will never happen'? A soldier without the will and desire to fight is almost useless. In A J Cronin's book *How Green was my Valley* he describes how a young boy in a Welsh mining village, going to school for the first time in a neighbouring valley, returns home having been thrashed by the school bully. His father sends for an old blind Welsh prizefighter called Dai Bando and asks him to make his son into a boxer. Dai Bando says 'I won't make him a boxer, I'll make him a fighter. There are many that call themselves boxers that are not fighters.'

This is the quality that the Commanding Officer of a front-line unit of all three services likes to find and develop in his men. Without it, all the technical skills and all the professional ability in the world are nothing. This does not mean that COs like to start wars. It means that if there is a fight on anywhere within striking distance he hopes that all his men will want to be in it, if possible before anyone else gets there. A famous example of this spirit is in the early life of the late Sir Winston Churchill, who, in a few years of peacetime soldiering, found his way into more campaigns than many of his contemporaries saw in a lifetime.

It is a difficult quality to develop in peacetime, or even to identify. Certainly it is not the cheap toughness of the thug. There was little of that kind of 'toughness', or even of indiscipline of other kinds in 45 Commando. It was over six months before I had to send a Marine to detention; and in all my time in Aden not one man was sentenced by Court Martial.

It is a quality that is developed indirectly. You work hard, of course, at all sides of the professional skill of the unit. You work equally hard at developing in each man a high pride in his own ability, and in the ability and reputation of the unit in every sphere – in exercises in the field, in the routine duties of guards and ceremonial, in sport: pride in troop against troop, company against company, and in the unit against all comers.

There is no particular reason why this should develop the fighting spirit, except the empirical one, that it has been found through generation after generation to do so. Perhaps it releases the inner fires and energies along channels that are easily diverted, when the moment comes, to release as the fighting spirit I have described.

This close pride gives cohesion too. The unit must have professional skill; but pride transmutes the technical skill of the unit into teamwork.

Training in war-time, though full of difficulties of its own, is in one way easy. You usually know the kind of operation you are training for, and the broad area where you will fight; and you often know the approximate date by which you must be ready. In peace-time service abroad, or in the Strategic Reserve, you never know. You might go anywhere, and you might have to do any one of a great number of things. The factory's assembly line must be ready to start moving at any time to produce any one of a variety of products.

This was the situation in the Middle East in 1963. There were no particular operations impending. There were British interests that might have to be protected, or treaty obligations that might have to be met. There was nothing to suggest that any one of these might 'break'. 45 Commando had not been employed operationally as a unit since the Kuwait crisis, two years earlier. There had been the usual crop of revolutions in the Middle East, and no doubt there would be more; but 45 Commando had remained training in Aden and might continue to do so indefinitely. Our job was to train.

You cannot keep a unit at high pitch for long without driving everyone mad. The usual system is to run a cycle of training, a kind of wave motion, with perhaps six months between the crests – steadily working up to a big exercise on a particular theme, then sliding down again for leave and relaxation.

In 45 Commando we had this unusual system whereby the whole unit remained in Aden and the individuals passed through on a one-year tour. This meant that we could not afford the slow wave motion. There were always new men to train. Every man came out with at least nine months basic training, so we were not too worried about their individual skills. However we were always re-training the team. This, coupled with the fact that we had to be ready at all times to do almost anything, meant that the wave motion often degenerated into a fast ripple. Still, the men had no families there, and little to distract them in Aden – the few girls there were tracked down by the longer-serving RAF and Army units well before the Marines reached them. With only a year to serve, the men of the unit were able and willing to train at a fast pace.

And train at a fast pace we did. We were not allowed to train in the mountains, but stretching westwards from Little Aden was a wide expanse of desert, with only the occasional fishing village and patch of cultivation. Much of it was featureless and offered little scope for training; but there was space, space to exercise the kind of fast-moving operation of war that I had in mind. And the space began on our doorstep.

The desert began just west of the small group of volcanic hills of Little Aden, at the point where the new military cantonment was being built at Falaise Camp. Here the desert was flat, and a sandy track ran in a straight line westwards to the horizon. Ten miles out it was crossed by another track, barely definable in parts, but known to us as the M1. This, running southwest to the coast, was a trading route, and one met camel trains, or ancient Arab Landrovers, gaily coloured and packed with Arabs, children, goats, stores and women to a degree that no designer had ever contemplated. The desert was almost featureless, occasional thirty-foot high dunes providing the only prominent ground. We learnt to know our exact position by such landmarks as 'Stones and Bones' (a camel's skeleton), 'Lionheart Wood' (an insignificant patch of scrub), and 'The Tallest Tree in Arabia', only six foot high but standing high on a dune, and visible for miles. There was little chance of getting lost in this desert. It had none of the vastness of the North African and other deserts, and there was always a distant mountain to give a 'fix'. But it had its interesting moments.

The M1 reached the sea twenty-five miles out from Little Aden. Here the desert was a little more interesting. A great stretch of sand-dunes came down to within a mile of the sea, there were broken patches of scrub and dunes, and a three mile stretch of salt flats. Beyond this again the desert stretched for twenty miles, featureless except for two small hills, to the foot of the extinct volcano, Jebel Karaz, rising 2,000 feet straight out of the desert. To the south was scrub, salt-flats and the sea; to the north, broken scrubby country and a pass through the volcanic hills, providing one of the best training areas I have seen.

The desert had space, and there was some variety in the ground, but it was no pleasure place in the summer. Shortly after I arrived, and before I was acclimatised and used to the desert, I went out to watch one of my companies on an exercise in the scrub south of Jebel Karaz, where they were preparing a defensive position against a tank attack. I arrived in the late afternoon after a hot and dusty journey, sweated as I walked round the company area, and was thankful when the scorching sun went down and we retired to rest to await the dawn attack. The night was hot, but tolerable if one didn't move; and as I lay on top of my sleeping bag enjoying the stillness of the desert and looking at the cloudless sky packed with stars, I decided that the desert was a fine and romantic place.

After a minute I felt a nip on my forehead and I killed my first sand-fly. Others came to investigate, and soon I was swatting silently but hard. I climbed into my sleeping bag and pulled it over my head, and climbed out again because of the heat. I tried my insect repellent, which discouraged some of the insects but aroused the others to frenzy; anyway by then they had got inside my clothes, and I was alternately swatting and scratching. The battle went on until the early hours of the morning, when I finally got to sleep, defeated and exhausted, to be awoken within half an hour by the sound of tanks and the beginning of the dawn attack.

'Paddy' Stevens leads his men on patrol

After the attack the sun came up, and I felt the heat for the first time – I had not felt it fully the day before, driving fast over the desert. I stood up, sat down, lit a cigarette and put it out immediately, started to drink water and put the mug down, stood up and walked about and sat down again to stop sweating – utterly uncomfortable, the body not yet adjusted to the heat and the sun. There are far worse deserts than Aden, but that was little consolation at the time. Of course one got used to this, as one can get used to almost anything, and I came to enjoy living in the desert, provided I could choose my spot. It was an acquired taste.

This was the area over which we were to train during the hot summer of 1963. There were many tasks to train for. We could be flown almost anywhere in the Middle East, or to do Internal Security (policing) duties, all in a variety of countryside – desert or jungle, mountain or plain, even perhaps in towns. We could not train for them all. I laid down that we would concentrate on training at troop level, primarily in the attack, and on 'battle procedure' – loosely, the drills for committing a unit to battle.

The first thing, though, was to make sure that Commando Headquarters was working efficiently and to get some practice myself. We carried out several exercises with HQ, setting up HQ in the desert by day and by night, moving again at night, all the while controlling imaginary battles by radio. The 'companies', represented by Landrovers with radios, sent in reports to give a battle picture, or occasionally such confusing reports that no picture appeared at all.

When I was satisfied with the running of HQ we extended the exercises to mobile radio battles, with most of the officers of the unit mounted in Landrovers with radios as we pursued an imaginary enemy across the desert – an optimistic concept perhaps, but it gave us all practice in speaking quickly and fluently over the radio, passing brief but accurate reports, giving and receiving orders and reacting quickly.

We held our first unit exercise at the end of August. It was the most unpleasant exercise I have ever known. We dug a defensive position near 'Lionheart Wood' fifteen miles from Little Aden, in dunes of fine sand. As we started to dig, a sand-storm blew up and continued for two days – not a bad one even by Aden standards, but enough to blow the fine sand into our ears and nose, on to the food one was eating, and filling up the slit trenches as quickly as they were dug. The combination of sand and heat tried our tempers, but eventually the wind died down and the defensive position was completed. That night we moved again and dug a new position.

All this was only a prelude. Everyone has a theory, and mine was briefly this: if British troops are committed to a limited war they will not be called in until the situation is almost beyond repair. The first troops to arrive will be outnumbered. Sometimes there may be nothing you can do except sit and defend until you are reinforced. But defence allows the enemy time to concentrate his greater strength, so that he can soon make reinforcement of any airhead or beach-head impossible. The best chance may often be to make use of the surprise of one's arrival and attack quickly to neutralise the main enemy within striking distance, and then to keep on attacking.

This, then, was the concept – attack, followed by re-grouping and other attacks in rapid succession, as swiftly as the battle procedure and logistics – and the enemy – would allow. There is nothing remarkable or new in that concept. It is a traditional one of amphibious warfare, often a necessity in that form of warfare; often neglected, with disastrous results. It would provide us with a theme, one that would be useful if we were called on to do an amphibious landing, and anyway a good basis for any kind of operation.

We needed the ability to move and deploy quickly, in vehicles or in helicopters or on foot, to attack quickly, and then to recover quickly so that we could move again. I had led up to this concept in the HQ exercises, and had warned the companies to train for it. In October we had the first opportunity to exercise it with the whole unit. We had no amphibious ships, and no aircraft were available to stage a 'fly in' to one of the airstrips along the coast. But the essence of the concept lay in fast movement and deployment. We had the desert, and our own transport, and some extra transport we borrowed from the RASC. 4th Royal Tank Regiment, our neighbours in Little Aden, provided a squadron of armoured cars; and 26 Squadron RAF, under Squadron Leader Peter Hart – of whom we were to see a great deal – provided two Belvederes.

We set off from Little Aden behind a screen of armoured cars, travelled forty miles over the desert and along the coast against a series of delaying battles, and in the late afternoon attacked, with strike aircraft in support, the first main enemy position. At first light we set off again in transport, moving fast over the desert, bypassing enemy for the rear company to isolate and destroy, and again in late afternoon carried out a Commando attack with strike aircraft in support; this time we used the Belvederes for the quick move of reserves. By last light we were established in the pass to the north of Jebel Karaz. We marched most of the night over broken country to secure a commanding hill five miles behind the enemy. Soon after first light we advanced again, on foot and more cautiously, coming up against the main enemy position in the afternoon. That night we attacked, over difficult and broken ground and up steep slopes, suffering one serious and four minor casualties in the process.

And that was enough for a while. It had been a hard exercise though a short one, and a fast pace; and the unit had shown it could move fast and deploy fast, both by day and by night. Companies were reacting quickly when they made contact, and reports were coming in to HQ quickly and accurately; and the re-supply had worked. All had not gone completely smoothly, and faults had appeared; but at least we knew what they were and could get them right. It was time for a rest.

These exercises took up a relatively small part of the unit's time, and a small part of my time as CO. In between, the companies carried out their own training and exercises, going into the desert for several days at a time or training near Little Aden, doing as much shooting and night training as possible. We were an 'air-transportable' unit, and had to carry out training and studies in this; and we had to keep our training in Internal Security continually up to date.

The cramped and aging camp at Little Aden caused constant administrative problems. The greatest of all these problems, and one with me throughout my time in Aden, was air-conditioning – far more necessary in these tiny rooms than is heating in an English house in the height of winter. Most of the air-conditioning machines had been installed many years before: in the words of my medical officer, they were suffering from 'advanced senile decay'. On my second day in the unit the air-conditioning in the largest hut broke down, and there was a three week battle to get it put right.

Conditions in the camp were not good. Much had been done over the last four years to improve it; but it was still a Spartan place, with almost no facilities for the men of the unit. The problem was always money. To make the camp a pleasant place would need a lot of money. Understandably, no-one would spend big money to improve a dying camp when new barracks were being built at Falaise three miles along the road. All our efforts to get things done met with a lot of sympathy – but not much money.

The Marines suffered most of all. They had their small huts; a primitive NAAFI bar with a covered patio; a WVS hut, a rough open-air cinema; and a large air-conditioned dining hall and good food. There was also the beach close by. But that was all. There was nothing for them in Little Aden outside the camp. Aden was 20 miles away, and though we ran trips there several times a week, very few men went – it wasn't worth the effort.

There was much sport, of course. Soccer, incredibly, was played through the heat of the summer; and there was hockey, basketball, cricket and other games. Much later we were given six fine canoes by the Nuffield Trust, and within a week the canoe club had thirty members. A month after I arrived we had a windfall, BP letting us take over a large air-conditioned shed inside our lines. This we turned into a Sports Centre, with badminton, judo, weight-lifting and various other devices we thought of from time to time. It all helped, but nothing could disguise the fact that the camp at Little Aden was not paradise.

The men adjusted themselves to this apparently barren life in an astonishing way, perhaps because, deprived of much else, they had to find their satisfactions in the life of the unit – in a way that would be impossible in a unit in Britain, with families there or the attractions of a nearby town. The men were in Aden for a year. Most of them sized up the situation pretty quickly, found themselves something to do, and settled in.

Most, though, preferred to be away from Little Aden. Company and unit exercises were welcome breaks from the camp routine. Occasionally we had to provide escorts for survey parties and other groups going into the mountains, which meant being away from camp for a week or two. This was always popular.

Most popular of all, and the nearest anyone found to paradise in Aden, was Dhala. Dhala is a State high in the mountains, ninety miles north of Aden State and on the

Yemen border. The capital of the State, Dhala town, is ten miles from the border and lies in a flat, broad valley surrounded by mountains. A battalion of the Federal Regular Army is stationed there; and there was a separate camp nearby for one company of the Commando. It is a striking place. 'Commando Camp' stands on a low flat hill in the middle of the valley: a tented camp with few amenities, and surrounded by a stone wall and sandbags and barbed wire. Nothing much apparently. But the air there is staggering after Aden. It is cool, even cold at times, and the water from a shower-bath hits you with the chilliness of a Highland stream. The scenery is magnificent. Much of the year the valley is green; and two miles to the west of the camp the Jebel Jihaf rises almost sheer in places for 1,600 feet to a plateau – a plateau even greener than the valley below, the air even more thrilling.

We sent each company to Dhala for three months at a time for training, and they trained very hard. The Jebel Jihaf provided a good morning's exercise, and there was a rifle range and a field firing range nearby.

Best of all were the patrols. Some policing was required in the hills around Dhala. Most of this was done by the FRA battalion, but frequently the company was invited to send patrols to remote villages.

Chapter 3

The Cool Season

Aden remained hot throughout September and most of October. During these months there was a noticeable shortness of temper – not among those like myself who had arrived quite recently (at least I thought not) but among the men who had suffered through the whole summer. I was told by an old hand of Aden that this was a seasonal hazard and would soon pass.

Sure enough; in late October the weather changed quickly; the wind seemed cooler, the sun no longer beat back off the sand and rocks and buildings with the same intensity, and tempers cooled. There was a lightening of spirits everywhere and we found new energy. Work and training became easier, we played harder, and Aden, at best tolerable in the late summer, became positively enjoyable, in parts. It was still hot, sometimes very hot, by English standards, perhaps the equivalent of a scorching English summer's day: we wore tropical dress throughout the winter: but it was tolerable, and the sea was near and the nights were cool.

We had worked through the heat of the summer, and now took a rest before the hard training of the cool season began – not leave but a general lessening of the tempo of work. Even so the days seemed to fill up quickly.

The cool season brought, in increasing numbers, what we irreverently called 'Visiting Firemen' – VIPs, staff officers and others from UK, come to see conditions in Aden and to discuss problems. Most of these were more than welcome – we were quite prepared to discuss our problems with anyone, at length. It was sensible for them to come in the cool season, for the pressure of their tours would have reduced them, in the hot season, to a pool of sweat.

One kind of Visiting Fireman, fortunately rare, was not appreciated – the man who came and said 'I thought Aden was hot. It's a nice climate. I wouldn't mind living here myself…'

Even in winter Aden was hot, for those who had to work in the sun.

One such Visiting Fireman had arrived and departed but left bitter memories; the bitterness was vented upon his unfortunate and innocent successors. There was no plan; it was only afterwards that we learnt what had happened. They visited a ship, and were taken into the engine room and kept there longer than was necessary for their purpose. They visited the tank regiment at Falaise, where a tank had been kept out in the sun since dawn with the engine running, and were dunked in the tank one by one. They visited us, and were walked up a high hill; they visited an Army unit nearby, and were kept talking in the hot cookhouse for some time: they were given similar treatment wherever they went. They took it all marvellously and earned our respect; and they learnt more about conditions in Aden than many who had been treated kindly.

Our rest did not last long. The Annual Inspection was due, when the GOC would descend with a team of experts to look into our efficiency. The unit was to parade equipped for an air move; after which the GOC would nominate different troops or troops of men to perform various tests, while his experts examined each corner of the unit's administration. There was a lot of hard work on preliminary inspections, searching for faults in our air-portability plans and in our administration and trying to divine what particular things the GOC would look for. An Annual Inspection is one of the less enjoyable parts of soldiering; but it was a chance to pull the administration together after the heavy training of the summer. The GOC arrived, some unexpected stones were turned over to reveal unexpected objects, but the inspection went well. The medical report read *'the morale of the unit reflect great credit on the officers and senior NCOs...'*

Meanwhile we trained; we gave a demonstration of a new anti-tank weapon; we held an officer's study period; we played games. There was a threat of trouble in Aden and we stopped everything; the threat passed, and again we trained. Always there was a constant stream of new men arriving and familiar faces leaving, always work to keep the ever-changing unit up to its old standards. It was like digging in fine sand, as in the summer exercise: we had to dig hard to stop the trench from filling in, let alone dig it deeper. Somehow, though, we seemed to be getting deeper.

For my part I watched training; I planned training for the future; I peered at Contingency Plans and put them away again; I faced a steady stream of officers from the unit with their administrative problems; I wrestled with paper in the office, always too much paper; and, as a facet of my duties, I found myself drawn into the quickly increasing tempo of the social life in Aden as the cool season advanced.

One day I remember in particular: orderly room, then a Visiting Fireman, a Study Period for the officers; a lunch with the visitors; watching the cross-country finals, then a quick dash to see the end of a soccer match; to the office to clear work left over from the morning; a fast drive to Aden to arrive, late, at an official reception; afterwards, a quick-change act in the car park into mess-kit and on to a regimental dinner, which lasted until the early morning. It was a long day, and there were many like it.

With the Annual Inspection behind us we turned again to hard training. I would have liked to have developed further the kind of fast-moving operation we had exercised in the summer. We needed variety, though; partly to hold the interest of the unit, even more because we had many different roles and must keep our minds and our techniques flexible.

It would be nice if we could divine what kind of operation, if any, we were most likely to be committed to. The fast-moving techniques were a sound basis and applicable to many things; but we needed a specific problem, a definite form of warfare, and one that seemed likely.

We had often looked with interest at the mountains, but we had never been allowed to train there, except near Dhala. They remained the operational province of the Federal Regular Army, and British troops would not be used there except in an emergency. Reading the Intelligence Reports I was convinced that one day we would be called upon to operate in the mountains. I was afraid that if the emergency came we would not be ready for it, untrained in the special arts of mountain warfare and unaccustomed to the peculiar mountains of the Federation. In November we began to prepare, tentatively, for mountain warfare.

I shall have much to say about the mountains later, but for the moment it is enough to say that they were high, hot and revolting – a mixture of volcanic rock and limestone, often crumbling in the hand or slipping away from under foot; knife-edge ridges; sheer cliffs where great slabs had fallen away split off by the heat, with steep scree slopes below. They were bare, very bare, and hot to the touch, and there was little water.

We had a small-scale model of these mountains on our doorstep at Little Aden, and this provided us with the nursery slopes. There was a scramble course – a run of ten or fifteen minutes (according to age) across the nearest hill, used by the Commando for several years. This we now used more often, setting times and encouraging it as a spare time hobby (which many took to), and later moving over it at night. Individual training was done in a rocky setting, then troop and company training, as we worked our way towards a unit exercise.

I told one of the company commanders to prepare a map exercise, a study period for the officers. He chose an area near Dhala (which, curiously, was the scene of an FRA battle nearly a year later), and in late November we examined the problems of movement in this strange country, the equipment we would need, and the appalling problem of re-supply, particularly of water.

In early December we held our first unit exercise in mountain warfare, in the great crater of Jebel Karaz, two miles across and filled with secondary hills. It was an elementary exercise, unrealistic in some ways, but it was useful. We moved out in transport, made the final approach – a march of several miles – at night on foot, and at first light were on high ground. We left picquets and observation posts there, and the companies moved on to secure a succession of hills. Spotting the enemy was difficult, even using light aircraft, but we eventually found and surrounded them, using Squadron Leader Peter Hart and his two Belvedere helicopters to move the reserves.

It was not the best of exercises. Much was artificial, and much would not have stood the test of real enemy. But it brought us face to face with the essential problems

– the difficulties of crossing this unpleasant country; the heat, even at night, and the amount of water we would need; and the difficulties of controlling a battle in a country where maps were misleading and inaccurate and radio often screened by the hills.

As a result of the study period and of this and a later exercise, and of discussions with FRA officers experienced in mountain warfare, we had the beginnings of a technique. Two things stood out. I had long believed in the tactical use of helicopters in the right circumstances. In these bare mountains, where helicopters could be seen and shot at from far away, and where landing sites for large helicopters were difficult to find, I doubted their value for landing troops on or near an objective, unless we had enough helicopters to be able to afford risks, or a wide area to choose from.

Secondly, I was convinced that we would have to operate by night. We held one short exercise later, in which we climbed steep hills in daylight: even with the kindest umpiring it was obvious that a long hot climb against steady shooting would be slow and costly.

Language was a great barrier, not only for operations in the mountains but also for our day-to-day contacts with the Arabs. British troops usually pick up a smattering of the local language quickly, and I had heard several strange but apparently fluent conversations between Marines and Arabs, punctuated on both sides by familiar English adjectives. This was hardly adequate even for our daily contacts or for the various small ways in which we tried to help the Arabs – repairing boats of the local fishermen, medical help at remote villages, a nearby youth club. It would be useless for interpreting on operations. We began an Arabic class, produced a phrase book, prepared tape recordings, and I never got beyond discussing the colour of My Motor Car; but some men took to it, and when the time came we had enough interpreters to see us through.

The December exercise was to be our last for a while, and we had planned a two month period to bring the individual training up to a high standard – shooting, weapon handling, fieldcraft and the many other military skills. This period was to culminate in a 'Subaltern's Day', in which every subaltern would be tested in his professional skills; and a long inter-troop test. Then we would be ready for the heavy programme of exercises planned for February and March.

By this time most of the officers who were to play their parts in the events of the coming year had joined. Major David Smith, a very experienced Commando, was second-in-command; X Company Commander was Major Mike Banks MBE, a well-known mountaineer and cliff-climber; Y Company, Captain Gavin Hamilton-Meikle, another experienced cliff-climber; Z Company, Major David Langley MC, and Support (mortars, machine guns etc.), Captain John Lloyd.

And by this time events had begun to take charge.

On 10 December, during our exercise at Jebel Karaz, a bomb was thrown at the High Commissioner at Khormaksar Airfield, killing two civilians and wounding several others. Because of this and other developments a State of Emergency was declared in Aden.

We drove at full speed over the desert back to Little Aden. We were not needed immediately, but we had to re-organise and re-train the unit for Internal Security duties. The threat of trouble in Aden rose and fell, and we rose and fell with it but never did anything except wait. An exercise was planned and cancelled. There was trouble on the Dhala Road in the mountains in an area called the Radfan.

Christmas came, a five-day break with all quiet in Aden. We celebrated, the sacred and the profane, and on Boxing Day the whole unit went for a run to shake their dinner down: we played six-a-side football; the officers played the sergeants at hockey and another indescribable game, in which we suffered and inflicted heavy casualties. We were glad to get back to work.

HMS *Centaur*, a strike carrier, arrived, delivered her helicopter squadron to operate with the Federal Regular Army in the Radfan, and went away again. We snatched a quick exercise with the squadron before they went up-country, and made friends with the pilots. New Year's Eve came, and we took over as Internal Security battalion, so that the King's Own Scottish Borderers could celebrate Hogmanay: again all was quiet in Aden.

1964 – the year of the 300th Anniversary of the founding of the Royal Marines. We wondered what fitting ceremony we could devise to celebrate the occasion.

On 2 January I spoke to the whole unit and told them that they could expect a hectic year. In a moment of blinding prophecy I told them that, whatever plans might exist for using us, they could bet their boots that we would go somewhere quite unexpected in a way that had not been planned at all.

January rumbled on. Another exercise was planned and cancelled. The Federal Regular Army began Operation Nutcracker, to defeat the dissidents in the Radfan who were interrupting traffic on the Dhala Road. I flew up to the Radfan and visited Lieutenant Colonel Roy Watson of FRA, who was commanding the operation, had a look at the landscape, and was glad to go away and leave it to him. HMS *Centaur* arrived again, deposited her Royal Marine detachment, and disappeared.

The Scots Guards arrived from Kenya for training, and we looked after their advance party and showed them round the desert. I offered Mike Banks' company as enemy for their big exercise, told him he was to be defeated five times in three days, and over-ruled his tortuous devices for wrecking the exercise. We won the Middle East Boxing Championship. We practised air-portability. We practised Internal Security. We practised everything in rapid succession as the barometer needle swung uneasily. I saw too many new faces around me, and with a kind of conditioned reflex I ordered another HQ exercise. The Subaltern's Test came, and – to the delight of the subalterns – was cancelled half-way through, because of an emergency that never developed.

The Band of 3rd Commando Brigade arrived from Singapore to provide us with six weeks martial music, ceremonial and light entertainment.

On the morning of 20 January I was called to HQ Middle East Command. I was told that the Tanganyika Rifles had mutinied, and I was ordered to embark the unit in HMS *Centaur* and sail at midnight for Africa.

My six months were up.

Chapter 4

Passage to Africa

HMS *Centaur*, a strike carrier commanded by Captain O H M St J Steiner RN, was at that time steaming fast towards Aden. We had had no previous contact with the ship. We had once, briefly, begun planning an embarkation in a strike carrier, but had had to drop the work because something more pressing had cropped up.

We were starting from scratch, and we hadn't got much time – just over twelve hours to get the men, stores and vehicles ready, move them twenty miles to Aden, and embark them. We had seventy tons of stores, twelve Landrovers and five Ferret Scout Cars of 16th/5th Lancers. The men were no trouble: their kit was all ready, and they just had to pack and go. The stores and vehicles were a different matter. They had to be taken to a jetty, put into a lighter, then taken out to the ship to be hoisted on board by a single crane. We had to move very fast indeed, packing the unit equipment and collecting stores from the various depots in Aden.

The first loaded vehicles left the unit lines an hour after the executive order, and working parties went with them to the jetty in Aden. Thereafter a stream of stores passed through our check-point at the jetty, the lighters arrived, and the long haul to the ship began.

I stayed at HQ Middle East, getting what intelligence I could about Tanganyika, occasionally driving down to the jetty to check progress. The Landrovers and Ferrets had gone early, but a great pile of stores remained, and the work went on long after dark. By 2130 hours the jetty was clear and I went on board.

There I found an astonishing sight. It would be unfair to call it chaos, for HMS Centaur and our advance party had planned soundly. But it was not tidy, and in the strange red glare of the flight-deck lights it seemed worse than it was.

45 Commando embarking in HMS *Centaur* at Aden prior to operations in Tanganyika

There were twenty large aircraft parked near the middle of the flight-deck. Peter Hart had arrived with two of his Belvedere helicopters. The Ferrets and Landrovers were being secured forward; and there were stores everywhere, in every clear space and among the aircraft and more being hoisted on board from the last lighters. They were jumbled almost hopelessly, hoisted out of the lighters in the fastest sequence rather than the orderly one; and officers and NCOs with working parties from various departments were burrowing through the piles, looking for their own familiar markings and carrying their prizes off to their allotted space on the flight-deck or below.

Marines of 45 Commando crowded into sleeping in the hangar of HMS *Centaur* during their passage.

The men, except the working parties, had come on board long before and had been taken into the after hangar. I looked down there from the flight-deck and saw row upon row of camp beds packed so tight that it seemed impossible to move between them. Incredibly they were settled in, and many of them were asleep already.

The wind had risen; and for a while it looked as though the embarkation would have to be stopped. Luckily the wind died again, the work went on, and just after midnight all the stores and working parties were reported on board. There was a mess still, but that would have to wait until tomorrow. The ship sailed, and I went to bed.

Early next day we began work. The first problem was the flight-deck. Somehow it had to be prepared for the launching of a helicopter assault. HMS *Centaur* had six Wessex helicopters of 815 Squadron (Lieutenant Commander R. Bluett RN) – anti-submarine helicopters, but they could be stripped to carry 8–12 men; and they had recently operated in the Radfan, and were not new to this kind of game. There were Peter Hart's two Belvederes,also fresh from the Radfan. The fixed wing aircraft, Vixens and Gannets, were normally stowed below in the two hangars; but with the hangar full of men many of them had to stay on the flight-deck. With the Ferrets, Landrovers and much of the unit stores on the flight-deck too, it was crowded.

HMS *Centaur* sorted this out very quickly. The fixed wing aircraft were concentrated amidships; the Ferrets and Landrovers were lined up on the starboard side of the flight-deck forward. This left room for three Wessex operating spots forward, the other Wessex being parked amidships or stowed below. The Belvederes, much larger helicopters, took up the after end of the flight-deck. The stores that could not be got below were stowed just forward of the 'island', with an overflow among the parked aircraft. We had brought 130 jerricans of petrol on board, for our own vehicles and for any we might borrow if we landed. These were greeted with horror by the ship's officers, because of the stringent fire precautions in a carrier. However space was found for them in a sponson on the side of the flight-deck, surrounded by sentries and fire-extinguishers.

On the first morning, too, we began planning. None of the ship's officers had had any experience of a helicopter assault; but it was a worked-up and efficient ship, and they tackled this strange task with remarkable energy and skill. The unit as a whole had had no training in Commando Ship operations. However most men had done helicopter training, many of the officers had studied the problems, and we had some who had recently served in a Commando ship and knew the techniques well.

We held a joint conference with the ship's officers and set up three joint planning teams – Assault, Communications and Intelligence.

The Assault Planning Team, chaired jointly by David Smith and the Commander (Air) – Kettle – had the biggest task of all. They were not concerned with the tactical plan – we hadn't got one anyway – but with the procedures for operating the helicopters and getting the unit ashore. In essence this is quite simple, if you are not expecting opposition. You can form the unit in the hangar in 'sticks' of, say, eight for a Wessex and sixteen for a Belvedere (so that sticks can be switched easily from one type of helicopter to the other), bring the sticks in groups up to the flight-deck on the lift, move them to waiting areas opposite the helicopters, and just pump them ashore in a steady stream.

In practice it is more complex, particularly if you have to land at more than one Landing Site or expect opposition. Helicopters occasionally go unserviceable, or are delayed on the deck for refuelling, or arrive back on board out of sequence. The unit, arranged in the hangar in the order you want it ashore, arrives there quite out of sequence, perhaps with key sticks missing. This does not matter much for a logistic lift, flying into a safe Landing Site, for time is not too important and you can sort the unit out later; for a tactical landing, where you may have to fight, or at least deploy immediately on landing, it is critical.

Aircraft and stores parked on the flight deck of HMS *Centaur* during the passage to East Africa, looking more like Farnborough Air Display

There is another problem in a tactical landing. Much depends on relative rates of build-up – the speed with which you can assemble a force at a given place compared with the speed with which the enemy can concentrate there. I shall have more to say of this later; for the moment it is enough to say that every pound of payload in the helicopter counts, every second in turn-round time on the deck and on the Landing Site. You cannot waste deck-space while a helicopter waits for a load of men or stores to be found or adjusted. The moment the helicopter touches down the men and the equipment, to the exact payload the helicopter can take, must be moving towards it.

All this requires careful procedures. The procedures we used were those of the Commando Ship, adjusted to the peculiar problems of a fixed-wing carrier. The basis was a 'stickorbat', a sheaf of papers in which the entire unit, men, stores and vehicles, was listed in the order in which it was required ashore, and divided into sticks.

The movement of men and stores was controlled jointly by David Smith and the Lieutenant Commander (Flying) from 'Flying Control', a greenhouse on the side of the island. Sticks were called forward on the hangar broadcast, they marched on to the lift and knelt down opposite their guides; when the lift reached the flight-deck the guides, directed by radio from Flying Control, led the sticks to their allotted waiting areas. Flying Control was getting continuous reports of the movement and availability of helicopters, and the flow of the unit could be adjusted at any time.

The Communications Planning Team produced the systems for controlling the flow of helicopters and for controlling the whole battle. The helicopters had a radio net to control them when they were joining or leaving the flight-deck; they switched to another to control them for their run to the coast; and to yet a third, controlled by a special radio landed with the first wave, to direct their movements close to the Landing Site.

The assault procedures and the communications plan enabled us to control an operation very closely – not only from the ship during the early stages: even after I landed I could control the flow into the Landing Sites and adjust the movement as the battle developed.

The Intelligence Planning Team was responsible for collecting and sorting all the hard facts and presenting them to the Captain and me, so that we could make our tactical plan. They had a difficult task, as we had surprisingly few facts. We had some maps of Tanganyika. We had routine information about the ports and the main airfield and some background about the capital, Dar-es-Salaam. We had no air photographs to enable us to assess Landing Sites; and no 'battle intelligence', no up-to-date information about the whereabouts of the likely opposition.

We knew some bare facts about the strength and equipment of the Tanganyika Rifles. We knew that the 1st Battalion was based at Colito Barracks, seven miles north of Dar-es-Salaam. We knew that they had mutinied, thrown out their British officers and appeared in the capital in large numbers, and that there had been rioting and violence in the capital. We did not know where they were now. Nor did we know what had happened to the 2nd Battalion, based on Tabora 340 miles inland, which had also mutinied and thrown out its officers, or the company at Natchingwea, 220 miles south of Dar-es-Salaam.

With so little to go on, planning was difficult. It was made more difficult by the fact that we did not know what, if anything, we would be required to do. Tanganyika was an independent country and had not asked for help. It had merely been a sensible precaution on someone's part to embark the unit in HMS *Centaur* and send it to steam off the coast in case there was a sudden call for help. 'What kind of help?' as Shakespeare said. We had a Commando, strike aircraft, helicopters, Ferret Scout Cars, anti-tank guns, riot equipment, tear gas, in fact the whole golf-bag on a trolley. We were ready for most things but we had no basis to plan on. Yet plan we must, in case the call came suddenly.

A helicopter assault is a highly technical business. I have mentioned the technique for ferrying a unit ashore. This is only part of it.

Much of the problem hangs on the vulnerability of helicopters. A helicopter trying to land close to an alerted and angry enemy is probably a dead duck. Helicopters have shown that they can take a remarkable number of bullets, even in the rotor blades, and still fly; but no helicopter yet designed can take accurate automatic fire at close range and have a reasonable chance of surviving, even if the men inside it are not hit.

The most vulnerable thing on the battlefield, though, is a soldier advancing on foot over open ground. He is more vulnerable if he is tired; he is vulnerable when road-bound in transport moving through enemy country. Whatever he does he takes risks.

The vulnerability of helicopters is a relative thing. Helicopters can fly at 100 knots or more, can fly over rivers, swamps, jungles or mountains, and arrive in unexpected places. The enemy cannot defend everywhere. There will often be places where he is unlikely to be: troops landed there by helicopter, fit and fresh, can launch a sudden attack or force the enemy to attack them on the ground they have chosen. If the routes are clear of enemy, if you have enough helicopters, if you have good intelligence of the ground and the enemy, you can consider a helicopter assault.

You do not normally attack the enemy directly in helicopters. As the Americans put it, 'you hit 'em where they ain't'.

The critical problem, though, is usually relative rates of build-up at the chosen spot, yours against the enemy's. You will seldom get enough helicopters to land a large force at one time, or even get a Landing Site big enough to land them all at once. You usually depend on a steady stream of helicopters into the Landing Site, with each helicopter doing several trips, perhaps half-an-hour between trips as it flies to and from the ship.

With fifteen Wessex you might get a company and its support weapons down in each lift. Depending on the distance it might take two hours or more to land the fighting part of the unit.

The moment the first wave touches down, even if there are no enemy there, surprise is lost and the enemy will do everything he can to bring troops, armoured cars, tanks and guns to bear on the Landing Site: when that happens your build-up slows or is stopped altogether just as the enemy's is increasing.

There are ways of delaying the enemy build-up, of course, such as deception plans or air strikes. Yet whenever a tactical landing is planned, this analysis of relative rates of build-up has to be made.

I have mentioned two types of helicopter landing: the logistic lift, to a safe Landing Site and where there is no desperate haste; and the tactical landing, where it is all haste and rapid build-up. There is a third kind, the 'coup de main' operation, a direct assault on a key position held by the enemy, such as a vital bridge. This is a risky business. It depends on complete surprise; it is usually done with only one wave of helicopters, at least until the coup de main party has cleared the area; you need accurate intelligence of the enemy and of the Landing Site; and you don't usually do it unless you have enough helicopters to be able to afford losses.

This should make our problem in HMS *Centaur* clearer. We had only eight helicopters, so we could not afford risks. We had a crowded flight deck, and were only partly trained, so we could not hope for a rapid build-up. And we had little information about the ground and even less about the opposition.

Clearly we would prefer a logistic lift if possible. We were capable of a tactical landing – with reservations – and planned for that from the start. The one thing we could not do was a coup de main operation.

With this theory as our basis we did what planning we could. We tried to guess what we might be asked to do – clear Dar-es-Salaam? Land north of the town to isolate Colito Barracks? Capture the airfield? Seal off the residential area? There were too many possibilities. We chose two and worked out contingency plans in detail. At least they provided the planners with batting practice.

One thing we considered briefly and discarded: a direct assault on Colito Barracks. That would amount to a coup de main operation. With our state of training, so few helicopters and no intelligence, it was unthinkable.

Our only real asset in planning was the technique of landing. To enable the planners to get down to detailed work I gave a standard landing plan for the unit. This was, simply, to land three company groups (rifle companies with their support weapons) in succession, each capable of securing, marking and controlling a separate Landing Site.

We had the ability to land. We had no tactical plan. We would have to await orders and facts. We were flexible. Very flexible.

All this planning had begun on the first day. Training began then too. The helicopter emplaning and deplaning drills were simple enough, but had to be worked over to cut down the seconds. On the second day at sea each company in turn ran through the whole assault procedure, and on the third and fourth days we held dress rehearsals for the whole unit.

Each morning and evening we held co-ordinating conferences, chaired jointly by the Commander (Air) and myself, at which the Intelligence Team ran through the latest intelligence and all teams reported progress. We then set the targets of planning and training to be done before the next meeting. Between these co-ordinating conferences were endless meetings to resolve technical problems.

HMS *Centaur* had rapidly turned herself into a Commando Ship. She was still a strike carrier, though, and at any time might be ordered to operate her fixed-wing aircraft. Catapulting them off was not difficult; but they had to be able to land again. This meant that all the aircraft on the flight deck had to be stowed in the after hangar. It also meant that the men had to move. We worked out a simple drill whereby every man picked up his bed and bedding, his rifle, his equipment and pack, put them on his head, and marched aft, to pack tight on the small quarter-deck or in the passage ways. We called this 'Sardine Stations'. We never practised it.

Four days went by quickly, and on 20 January we were steaming far off the coast of Tanganyika, waiting. There was still much to be done, but we felt that more or less ready. There was no call for help and not much news. What news there was suggested that all was quiet in Tanganyika. We waited and we thought we would be ordered back to Aden.

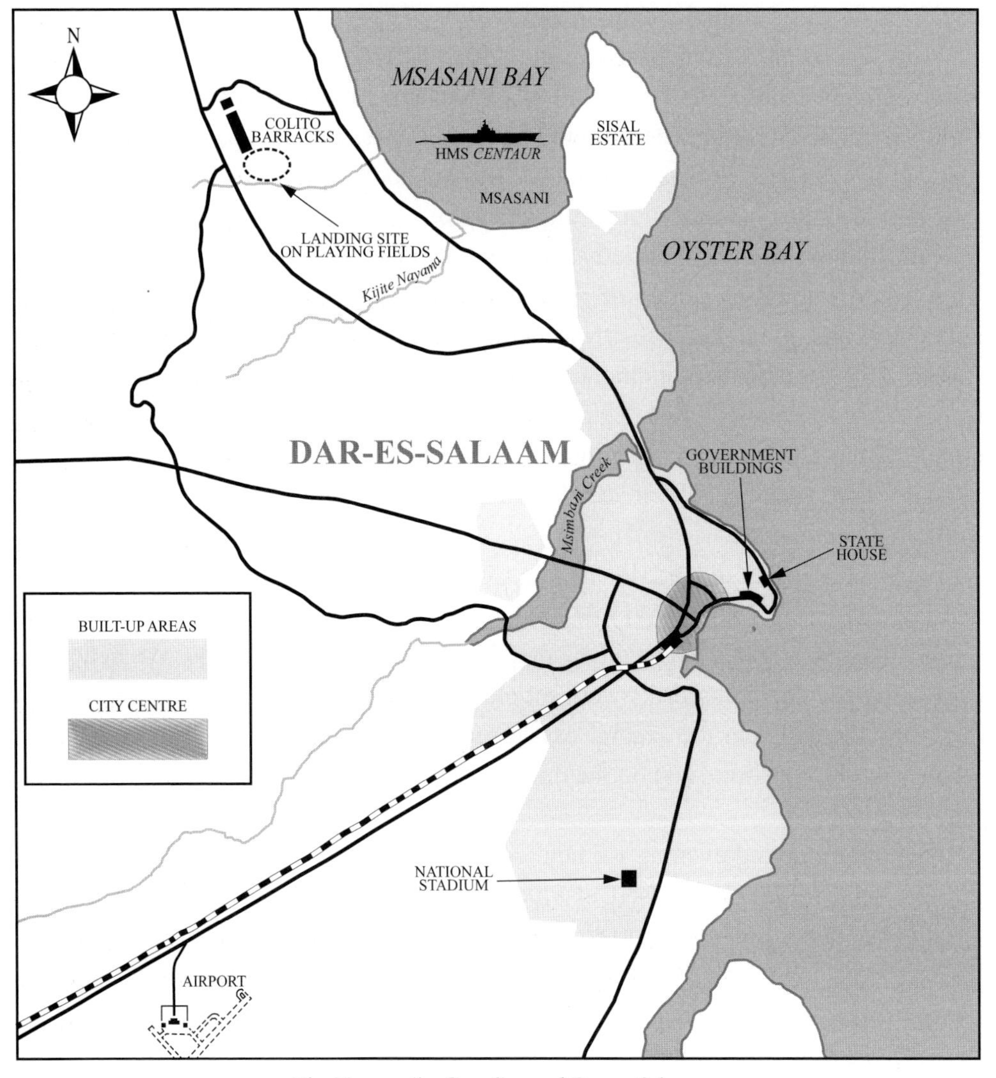

The Tanganyika Coastline and Dar-es-Salaam

Chapter 5

Tanganyika

The 24 January had been a busy day, with rehearsals, conferences, many problems still being resolved. I got to bed at midnight, very tired. I put my light out, and a minute later there was a knock on the door and a messenger told me that I was wanted on the bridge. There Captain Steiner showed me two signals: the first, in the Nelson style, told us to 'proceed with all despatch to Dar-es-Salaam' to support the Tanganyika Government in putting down the mutiny; the second, with a touch of James Bond, told us to send a boat secretly to pick up an unknown VIP from a jetty near Dar-es-Salaam.

We let the unit sleep on; they might have a busy day ahead; and we speculated on who the VIP might be. Captain Steiner put his money on Brigadier P S Douglas, the former British commander of the Tanganyika Rifles, who had vanished at the time of the mutiny.

He was right. The ship was darkened, we closed the coast and at 0200 hours the ship's boat brought on board Brigadier Douglas and his GSO2, Major Brian Marciandi, tired and wet. They had been in hiding since the mutiny, but that day they had been in touch with the Tanganyika Government. They had then had an alarming two hours near the jetty, with soldiers patrolling nearby, until the ship's boat was brought in by signals from a torch.

In a small and dimly lit cabin under the bridge Brigadier Douglas gave us our first real intelligence of the situation ashore and our instructions from the Tanganyika Government. The troubles still continued, but most men of the battalion returned nightly to their barracks at Colito. Our first task was to disarm this battalion, and he recommended a direct approach. He warned us that many of the men would have their arms and ammunition on them. He also stressed that casualties to the mutineers must be kept to the minimum, and said that many of the soldier's families were living in the barracks.

It was a tall order.

We looked at our map and at some sketches that Brigadier Douglas had brought with him, and found ourselves with two choices. The barracks itself had scrub and plantation around it, and high ground and more scrub to the west. There were very few Landing Sites. Two miles to the south was a stretch of open country between the roads. This provided a good Landing Site, and we could build up the unit there and attack as soon as the unit was at full strength. However this would give the mutineers time to get organised, and time to attack the Landing Site, or at least bring fire on to it and so disrupt our build-up. There might be a pitched battle and casualties, which was exactly what we had been invited to avoid.

The other alternative was the football pitch along the south side of the barracks. This was ridiculous. It was a large and level Landing Site; but it was in direct view of the barracks, and some of the buildings were right alongside it. It would need only a few alert and resolute men to hit the first wave, destroy the first wave and disrupt the operation altogether.

We might just get away with it by a surprise landing at first light, if we moved fast after landing and gave the mutineers no time at all. The need to avoid casualties to the mutineers and their families was paramount, for every political and moral reason.

We decided on a coup de main operation, a direct assault on Colito at dawn, landing on the football pitch.

By the time we had finished our discussion we had only three hours left before dawn, for detailed planning, briefing the unit and going through the whole procedure of Assault Stations. We called the officers; and at 0315 hours, as the rest of the ship and the unit was being called, I held my O Group in the Admiral's dining cabin aft. The orders were brief, as we were using the standard landing plan. I described the situation ashore and the details of the ground, gave the company commanders their tasks, and made snap modifications to the landing plan. There was no time to prepare fancy plans of encirclement, even if our state of training had permitted it. We would ram the whole unit into the football pitch and operate from there. Wise virgins, we had a switch Landing Site to the south in case of trouble.

David Langley and Z Company were to lead. I told him to deploy fast to secure the Landing Site, and then to attack the guard-room on the left side of the camp, to seize the armoury and so prevent a prolonged fight from developing. Above all, an attack there should divert attention away from the Landing Site. I told him that he must get inside the camp gates even if it cost him half a troop to do it.

Tac HQ, S and Y Companies would follow in that order. Our mortars and machine guns would not be much use to us as we would be too close to use them. I struck them out of the landing plan and told John Lloyd to concentrate Support Company as a reserve, ready to land either as a rifle company or with their support weapons – or, if need be – with riot equipment.

Brigadier Douglas decided to land in the first wave; his knowledge of the ground and of the language would help a lot. We gave him a loudhailer, a pistol and a life belt.

The O Group broke up; Commander Kettle and the Squadron Commanders went off to complete their own plans, and the whole team, ship, squadrons and unit, prepared for landing. The after hangar became a scene of confusion, with camp beds and bedding being stowed, officers giving their orders and men sorting their equipment. At 0515 hours the ship went to Assault Stations, and the confusion in the hangar dissolved into rows of waiting men. With the ship darkened, HMS *Centaur* approached the coast.

I went up to the bridge to wait until my stick was called, so as to be with Captain Steiner if we had to make any rapid changes of plan. On the flight deck, in the red glow of the deck lights, helicopters were being wheeled into position and the first sticks of Commandos were filing past the strike aircraft and piles of stores to their waiting positions. Just after 0600 hours the first grey light spread in the sky behind us, revealing the coast and our landmarks near Colito Barracks. The helicopters started up, the first sticks doubled forward, and they were away, low over the dark sea.

This was the worst moment of all. There were too many unknown factors. We knew little about what the other side were doing: we did not know what, if anything, they knew about us – whether they knew we were there, and had somehow been warned that we were to land somewhere, whether they had even seen the dark outline of HMS *Centaur* as she steamed right into Msasani Bay, and were standing to, ready to receive us. In attempting to finish the mutiny in a single blow we had staked everything on the assumption that we would take them by surprise.

The Landing Site at Colito as seen from the barracks

Our imaginations pictured armed men tumbling out of the barrack blocks as they heard the approaching helicopters. We could see the helicopters against the grey sky as they gained height crossing the coast so as to spot their Landing Site. They crossed well south of Colito and turned north to run in up-wind, then dipped out of our sight against the black background of hills. We watched anxiously for the flare of burning helicopters.

The 'landing reports' came in by radio, in quick succession from the helicopters, from Z Company and from the Control Team landed with the first wave. We had achieved complete surprise. After a few moments we heard the drone of the helicopters of the first wave returning to the ship. The second sticks of Commandos were already at their waiting positions as I nipped down to the Assault Operations Room below the bridge. The latest reports from Z Company confirmed that they had achieved surprise, and said that they were securing the Landing Site.

Commando HQ was to land immediately after Z Company, so I pulled on my kit and went down to join my stick at its waiting position on the flight deck. Final reports were passed to me saying that all was well; we doubled forward to the helicopter and were off.

When we touched down it was light, and very noisy. We had arranged for a display of fire-power to intimidate the mutineers: HMS *Cambrian*, a frigate, was firing air-burst shells high over a sisal estate to the north, and David Langley's rocket launchers were blasting away at open ground on either side of the camp. Scattered rifle shots were coming over the Landing Site; but none of the helicopters was hit, and the troop defending the Landing Site now moved right into the edge of the barracks.

As we had hoped, the main noise was coming from our left, near the barrack entrance on the main road west of Colito. Lieutenant Ian Martin had led his troop away quickly, followed by David Langley and Brigadier Douglas. Near the guard room they came under fire; but Ian Martin, a young subaltern in action for the first time, led his troop skilfully, returned the fire and closed in. Brigadier Douglas then addressed the mutineers in Swahili through his loudhailer, calling on them to surrender. They refused; he gave them a ten-second countdown, and at the end a rocket-launcher bomb was fired, hitting the roof of the guardroom. Firing stopped, the mutineers began to surrender, and Z Company entered the camp from the west. It was just before 0700 hours.

At the Landing Site the build-up was continuing rapidly. X Company arrived – but no Mike Banks. I deployed one of his troops to cover the eastern exits of the camp. Gavin Hamilton-Meikle arrived with Y Company but still no Mike Banks. I sent Y Company off to block the roads leading south and to secure the high ground to the west of the camp, retaining one troop as a reserve to be moved by helicopter. Helicopters released from the airlift were already searching the ground to the north of the barracks.

We got all three companies into the Landing Site in seventy minutes – a remarkable performance by the ship and the squadrons with so few helicopters. We even got Mike

Banks – sour: his helicopter had gone unserviceable after take-off and he had had to return to the ship to get another.

I had a quick chat with David Langley and Gavin on the radio, ordered David to search the west half of the camp and told Mike to take the east half. I then went forward to join David Langley and Brigadier Douglas at the guardroom.

The mutineers were surrendering now in large numbers and handing in their arms. The mutineers had several casualties: we got these to the Landing Site, where the stream of helicopters was still bringing in our stores and the rest of HQ, and they were flown back to the ship and given medical treatment.

At the guardroom about 200 Askaris were sitting in a group and more were being brought in. The mutiny of this battalion was virtually over. This was a big barracks though, and it took time to search it and round up the stragglers. A few escaped to the north: one group was shepherded in by helicopter, the pilot waving his pistol out of the window.

Escorting a group of Askaris who had surrendered

While this was going on Brigadier Douglas got in touch with the Government in Dar-es-Salaam by telephone and told them what was going on. He told me that he wanted to get there as quickly as possible. We had helicopters on reconnaissance over the city and the airfield, and from these and other sources we learnt that there were armed groups at both places. It was time to move on.

Our twelve Landrovers had arrived by Belvedere. We had also flown in some drivers with each company, and we now borrowed the transport of the 1st Battalion. The keys of their trucks had disappeared, but the Vehicle Mechanics landed with HQ soon put the trucks in running order. I told David Langley to take over the barracks with Z Company, concentrated X and Y Companies, and sent a warning to the ship that I would shortly need all the helicopters again.

I allotted the helicopters to Mike Banks and told him to secure the airfield, where armed men were reported to be holding hostages and demanding an aeroplane. We had previously made a plan for the capture of the airfield, and this he now carried out. He set off in great style at 1000 hours with all the Wessex and Belvederes and the two air-sea rescue Whirlwinds. He landed tactically, deployed quickly and moved in on the airport buildings – to be met by a beaming airport manager. The armed men had just left, so Mike put guards on the buildings, requisitioned vehicles and sent a patrol along the road to Dar-es-Salaam to look for the armed men and to secure certain key buildings.

Meanwhile we had got Commando HQ and Y Company into the vehicles; and we set off with Brigadier Douglas. The drive began tactically, with a helicopter reconnoitring ahead of us. It ended as a triumphal progress through the broad streets and high white buildings of Dar-es-Salaam, with Arabs, Europeans, Indians and Africans waving as we passed – all no doubt relieved that the tension was over. We reached the office of the British High Commissioner, and heard there of armed groups still in the town. I told Y Company to round up the armed men – which they did, quickly and without trouble – and to secure some key places in Dar-es-Salaam, and went in with Brigadier Douglas to see the High Commissioner. HMS *Centaur*, ever a jump ahead, had steamed round to Dar-es-Salaam and got hold of a lighter; she was now preparing to land the Ferrets, together with the ship's RM Detachment and a platoon of seamen.

Just after mid-day Brigadier Douglas gave me my next task, to deal with the 2nd Battalion, at Tabora 340 miles up-country. Latest reports were that they had handed in their arms when they had heard of the events at Colito. However the barracks was quite near the airfield. If a few resolute armed men changed their minds they could keep us out of the airfield, and the operation would develop into a long-drawn struggle, advancing up the main road. We decided to get there quickly and in style.

I needed two companies for Tabora. I could not leave Dar-es-Salaam empty, as the mood there was still uneasy and there were rumours that strikes and other troubles had been planned for that day. The Ferrets, the Seamen and the Ship's RM Detachment were already landing. John Lloyd and Support Company, organised as a rifle company, were now flown by helicopter direct into Dar-es-Salaam, bringing their riot equipment with them in case of emergencies. I called in David Smith to take command in Dar-es-Salaam and Colito, and set off for the airfield with Tac HQ and Y Company to join X Company.

Beverley transport aircraft had been asked for from Nairobi and were already on their way. Every minute counted, and a DC4 of the Williamson Diamond Mine Company was found and made ready by 1500 hours. The crew of the DC4 entered into the business with zest, and rigged eight ropes at the doors of the DC4 so that we could throw them out and make a quick exit when we reached Tabora.

There was no time for detailed orders. I told Mike Banks to bring on X Company as soon as the Beverleys arrived, and piled into the DC4 with Gavin and 54 men of Y Company. We did our planning in the aircraft. We had only a poor street map of Tabora, showing neither the airfield nor the barracks; but we would have to worry about that when we got there. We worked on the only assumption we could, that there would be shooting at the airfield even before we got out of the plane. The pilot would stop the aircraft close to the scrub at the edge of the airfield, and we would get out quickly and rush the airport buildings.

HMS *Centaur* had cleared the remaining stores of 45 Commando off her flight deck, with unconcealed delight, and was ready to resume her strike role. 340 miles was extreme range; but by manoeuvring at speed close to the coast she could fly off the Vixens with enough fuel to give them 15 minutes over Tabora. They were to arrive just before we did, to shoot us in or to support us after we landed.

We saw them overhead as we approached Tabora. We were silent, very tense, wondering how quickly we could get out of the DC4 if it was hit and burst into flames. I decided that this was one of those special occasions when a Commanding Officer should lead the way out, and stationed myself close to a door.

As we came in to land we saw an Argosy approaching the opposite end of the runway. The pilot, who had made contact with the control tower, gave a demonstration of the fastest and sharpest voice procedure I have ever heard; but the Argosy won and landed first, and we swept above it, to land a minute later. There we found some men of the RAF Regiment, sent from Nairobi with the same idea as we had – to seize the airfield quickly. It was most commendable, but it had ruined our entrance.

I had been told to consult the political authorities at Tabora before taking any action. They were at the airfield to meet me, with Captain Sarakikya, the new African CO of the battalion. The advice they gave was clear: the battalion was quiet, the arms were locked in the armoury, and the best thing we could do would be to stay at the airfield and not precipitate trouble.

However the arms were guarded by the men of the battalion; the ringleaders had not been arrested, nor were there any plans for doing this.

Mike Banks and X Company and the rest of Y Company had arrived. As it was getting dark I cut short the conference and went for a reconnaissance of the town and barracks with Sarakikya. On my return I rang Brigadier Douglas at Dar-es-Salaam and told him the situation. He told me to secure the arms and ammunition that night.

The airfield was crowded with salesmen and lookers-on, so I ordered the companies to give the appearance of settling in for the night. We stood to again at midnight, and Landrovers and trucks were brought in by the police and some local firms. We set off, with lights dimmed at first and then out altogether, and halted a mile from the barracks. As the companies moved forward in the darkness in single file along the grass verge, Mike Banks, Sarakikya and a section of men drove up to the guardroom in a Fiat and a civilian Landrover and silenced the guard. X Company moved in quietly and secured the armoury and magazines. No alarm had been given.

Y Company deployed quietly to surround the living area of the barracks. Sarakikya went into the living quarters with a bugler, sounded the general assembly, and told the battalion through a loudhailer they were surrounded, and ordered them to fall in on the main parade.

We had placed two Landrovers with headlights crossing on the parade ground, with men of X Company just visible in the shadows beyond. The battalion slowly gathered. Sarakikya stood alone in front of them, a commanding figure, and called out the names of the ringleaders. They came forward reluctantly at first: at a sharp order from Sarakikya they fell in smartly. Another order, an escort from X Company doubled forward into the light, and the ringleaders were marched away. The battalion faded into the darkness.

We finished piling the arms and ammunition into the lorries. I left Y Company in the barracks for the night and returned to the airfield with X Company. I reported to Brigadier Douglas, recommended that one company should remain at Tabora for a while, and turned in. It was 0400 hours, just twenty-two hours after our landing at Colito, which seemed a long time ago. We were very tired. For many of us it was our first rest of any kind for nearly two days.

We were up early next morning, and at 0800 hours Brigadier Douglas rang and told me to return to Dar-es-Salaam with one company, as another operation was impending. I held final meetings with Sarakikya and the political authorities, detailed Mike Banks and his company to stay at Tabora, and flew down to Dar-es-Salaam in a Pembroke that had appeared out of the blue.

Everything was in fine order at Dar-es-Salaam. The previous day David Langley at Colito had rounded up the remaining stragglers from 1st Battalion, and in conjunction with the African CO – a former student of his at Eaton Hall OCS – had begun to restore order and discipline. S Company had also helped with the rounding up, with helicopter patrols into the bush country. One such patrol, the anti-tank troop led by John Lloyd himself, had roped down from a helicopter virtually on top of six armed mutineers and captured them all. John found that the helicopter could not land anywhere near, and had a long walk home.

Patrols of Ferrets and troops had been sent round the town checking reports of armed men and providing a show of strength in likely trouble spots: the Ferrets were particularly impressive. On that first evening Brigadier Douglas and David Smith had led S Company, HMS *Centaur*'s Naval platoon and RM Detachment and the Ferrets in a 'flag march' through the town – a triumphal progress. As a final neat gesture, Captain Steiner had landed his Royal Marine Band, to play on the sea front and help in the steady return to normality and calmness.

David Smith took me to the National Stadium just outside Dar-es-Salaam, where most of the Commando was now based. I found it bedecked with flags – a nice gesture, I thought, until I learned that they were intended for Mr Chou-en-Lai, who was due to address a youth rally there. This, unfortunately, had to be cancelled.

There was a lot of work still to be done. There were many administrative headaches: these I left in David Smith's good hands. I saw Brigadier Douglas and got a brief for the next operation. I then went out to HMS *Centaur* to see Captain Steiner and discuss the many joint problems and to send a joint report back to HQ Middle East. There was also the detailed planning for the next day's operation. There was much to do. I got to bed at four o'clock again, and I was not the last.

Early next morning, the 27th, we had a final co-ordinating conference for the last operation. One company of the Tabora battalion was at Natchingwea, 220 miles south of Dar-es-Salaam. They had mutinied, but they too had handed in their arms. However their camp was right alongside the airstrip, and a setback at this stage would have proved disastrous. This, too, must be done in style.

I gave the job to Gavin Hamilton-Meikle and Y Company, with two Beverleys. 15 minutes before touchdown a radio message was sent to the company at Natchingwea telling them to fall in on parade. The airstrip was east of the camp: as a minor deception plan, in case any of the mutineers decided to give trouble, they were told that the landing would be by helicopter on the open ground to the west – we assumed that they would not make the calculations about payload and range. At the same time Vixens from HMS *Centaur* arrived overhead and reconnoitred the camp and airfield, sending continuous reports direct to the Beverleys carrying Y Company.

Y Company touched down on time, made a fast exit, surrounded the camp, and secured the armoury. By early afternoon they were on their way back to Dar-es-Salaam with the arms, ammunition and ringleaders.

I received Gavin's report by radio that all was well, and suddenly felt hungry. I had not eaten for two and a half days except for some biscuits and a sandwich. This was partly my own fault, partly my MOA's (Marine Officer's Attendant, or batman). He was always cheerful, but he had an unfortunate habit of producing lukewarm 'spaghetti-in-tomato-sauce' and stale tea whenever I wanted to eat; by the time he had done better we were on the move again. I went to a hotel and had a good lunch.

TANGANYIKA

MEMO.

From David C.O

To Paddy

30 Jan 1964

You will bloody well get 14 hours sleep a.s.p. You will show this to your 2/c who will be sacked if you don't

Orders to a Commanding Officer

Chapter 6

The Force in Readiness

Africa was full of troubles. In Kenya and in Uganda the armies had mutinied, the new democracies were shaken, and for a few days it looked as though East Africa might go the way of the Congo. In these places, as in Tanganyika, British troops moved in and disarmed the mutineers, with few casualties. Order was restored, and the British disappeared again. The surface rippled and heaved for a while from the swirling in the deep, then it subsided to calmness, or as near calmness as any part of the world ever gets.

The British troops had appeared suddenly and done their jobs as if they had been preparing for it. Transport aircraft had arrived quickly as if they had never had anything to do but wait on the runways. The ships might have been dawdling off the coast for months for just that purpose. It had all been very neat.

Neat? I have never known a military operation that was neat, seen from the inside. There is always confusion somewhere, or doubt, or the occasional frightening miscalculation. We had had our share – the chaotic embarkation, the worst I have ever known; moments of dismay while working against time to prepare for an unknown task; doubt at the moment of landing; confusion when we lost radio touch with the ship at a critical moment. We had had our problems, and had resolved them as they came.

When I read a military account that suggests perfect slickness, an elegant perfection, I wonder what difficulties have been glossed over, or whether there were any difficulties at all, so that the operation was not worth the study. Even a training exercise that goes too slickly suggests a poor exercise, too easy for the state of training, not pushed near the limits of the unit's readiness for war. Military operations are not like that; and the reasons are not difficult to see.

If there is an enemy, the enemy will not stay to fight unless he believes that he has some chance of winning, or at least of creating difficulties for the other side. If the opposition was slight, as it was in our case – though we did not know it at the time – there are problems of time and space, the need to finish everything before the other side can react, or before there are political developments.

'...Though we did not know it at the time...' This of course is the crux. You never know all the things you want to know – where the enemy is and how strong he is; what he is doing; what he is thinking, and how he is feeling; what he knows about you; exactly what the ground is like or what the weather will be like at the critical moment; and a thousand other things. You do not know. You collect what facts you can and sort them into a pattern of some kind. Too often the facts you get are a miserable lot, and you can make any pattern you like according to your taste and prejudice. Too often you find yourself with alternatives neatly balanced. There is nothing left for the commander to do but follow a hunch, collect all the kit he can and jump on to one side of the scale to bring it down with a bang.

After the operation has begun there are moments when the whole thing seems about to grind to a halt. The enemy has done something unexpected, or there are unexpected difficulties on the ground or the weather or in re-supply. The difficulties are often real, often imagined, the latter particularly when officers and men are tired. Calm analysis is no use, as there are no facts to analyse, only confused reports of difficulties. You have to trust to intuition, an indefinable feeling of what is really happening beyond the muddle. It is often best to give another shove, and trust that the unit is so schooled that everyone gives another shove all the way down the line to the youngest man.

This was the first time in my military life that I had had to make, in conjunction with others, a big decision. If we had made a mess of the landing the consequences throughout Africa could have been great; and we were thinking of landing, not cautiously as we might have done, but right on the doorstep. Luckily time made the decision for us – or lack of time. We had been told to go: it was obviously best to go at first light: it was obviously best to go straight in, to prevent a drawn-out battle. There was no time to meditate upon the future of Africa. We just went: but there were some horrible moments as the first helicopters turned towards the Landing Site.

Anyway it had worked. We had got on wonderfully with HMS *Centaur* from the moment we had arrived on board, we had been made welcome in a marvellous way, and we had resolved all our problems together. The unit had done well; obstacles had been thumped out of the way; and what had impressed me most was the speed with which everyone had reacted to strange situations in a strange place. Our tails were right up.

The job for which we had been invited into Tanganyika was done. We read our duty now as being to fade into the background, but immediately ready in case we were needed, and showing enough evidence of our readiness to discourage troublemakers. HMS *Centaur* stayed just outside the harbour, helicopters flew over the town, the unit remained in the National Stadium. Within the Stadium we prepared for any new call that might come. Batons and shields were landed, tear gas pistols were checked, and riot drill was exercised. One company was always at immediate readiness, another could be ready quickly, and transport was there for both of them. The seamen and RM Detachment from HMS *Centaur* remained with us and took their turn.

Outside the Stadium patrols of Marines in Landrovers, escorted by Ferrets, moved with studied nonchalance on carefully planned routes, their radios in contact with the Command Post in the Stadium. The Royal Marines Band landed daily to play bright music or to Beat Retreat. We played football. Each day we allowed a few more Marines on 'shore leave' into the town. Each day the tension eased.

One day Brigadier Douglas took Captain Steiner and me to meet President Nyerere. The whole Cabinet was there, we talked for an hour, and at the end the President formally thanked us and presented us each with an ebony and ivory fruit bowl and a signed photograph.

The process known as 'baron strangling' began. I don't know the exact meaning or derivation; it has something to do with accepting with relish the hospitality of the locals. Much hospitality was offered. At first we could only accept a small part because of our state of readiness. We made plans for steady development.

It was too good to last. During one of my visits to HMS *Centaur* Captain Steiner showed me a signal indicating that we might be moved out. He suggested that I fly to Nairobi. I said I hadn't got an aeroplane. He said what did I think aircraft carriers were for? And before I could protest I was poured into flying kit, strapped up with Mae West, dinghy and bone dome, stuffed into a Gannet with a few last instructions about safety drills, and fired off from the catapult, in the cramped observer's seat surrounded by meaningless dials and radar screens.

At Nairobi we learnt that we were likely to be relieved by 41 Commando, who had been flown to Nairobi from England, and that we were to re-embark and be held as a floating reserve again. To make it interesting we were to be embarked in a different carrier, HMS *Victorious*, as HMS *Centaur* was needed elsewhere. A new ship and a new helicopter squadron: we couldn't bear the thought of it. We had made a lot of friends in HMS *Centaur*.

We had no executive order to move, but, with memories of that terrible embarkation at Aden behind us, we jumped the gun, and concentrated our stores and began to move them to the jetty. This had to be done discreetly. There was still uneasiness in the town, and we did not want to give the impression as such a time that we were leaving Tanganyika empty. The patrols continued, helicopters still flew over the town, the band still played.

I had to warn Mike Banks at Tabora by telephone This was difficult, as anyone could listen in.

'Mike, I think you've had long enough stuck up there at Tabora. I'm going to change the companies round tomorrow and give you a run down here.'

'You needn't bother really, colonel, we're quite happy up here'

'Mike, I think it's best. There are a lot of good reasons.'

'We'd much rather stay. To be perfectly honest we're thoroughly enjoying it up here. There's a swimming pool and we're getting on well with everyone and we've made a lot of friends… etc, etc.'

Baron Strangling!

'Mike, Nick and his boys will be relieving you. You remember NICK? (CO of 41 Commando)'.

'Oh… I see… Oh.'

He had got the message.

The order to move came soon after. 41 Commando began to arrive by air. HMS *Victorious* arrived; the vehicles and stores were embarked, and during the afternoon the helicopters of the new squadron, 814, descended into the stadium to pick up the men. We need not have worried. They worked as deftly as if they had been carrying troops all their lives. They picked up Z Company direct from Colito Barracks equally deftly, and as a final touch they collected X Company, who had arrived at Dar-es-Salaam airfield at dusk, and flew them on board at night.

We would have liked some rest, a pleasant sea voyage. East Africa was still uneasy, though, and we had been embarked as a 'force in readiness', at short notice to land again. We had a new ship and a new squadron – a new team to fit into. We would have to get our rest later. Next morning, early, we set to work.

HMS *Victorious* (Captain P M Compston RN) had had three days to prepare for this task. The ship's officers had already roughed out an Assault Organisation, and when David Smith got on board he found that their ideas fitted neatly into ours. We set up the same planning teams as before and we began training and rehearsals. With our experience in HMS *Centaur* behind us we moved all the faster and we could have carried out a competent landing thirty-six hours after embarking – and no doubt an incompetent one earlier if needed. We were soon back to the standards we had reached in HMS *Centaur*.

There was no stopping at old standards, though. Those standards had been the best we could reach in four days – a good best as it turned out. But the luck had run with us and the opposition had been slight. Even more than before we did not know what, if anything, we would be required to do. It might be something far more difficult, and the luck might break the other way. We had been happy amateurs. The amateur rehearses until he gets his lines right: the professional rehearses until he cannot get them wrong. We had to become professionals.

We rehearsed the same old drills and procedures, rehearsed them until everyone was sick of them. The planners planned, as best they could, and we soon produced many refinements on our old procedures.

And of course we made Contingency Plans. Contingency Planning is a permanent part of peacetime service. You do not know what you will be required to do, so you try to guess, and often plan in some detail. I had long had a theory about Contingency Planning, and experience in the Middle East confirmed it. I believe it is Parkinson's Third Law that runs to the effect that, when a firm builds a marvellous new block for its central offices, it is a sign that the firm is on the decline. There is a kind of Parkinson's

Third Law in contingency planning. A contingency appears, and you begin to plan for it. As soon as your plan is complete, the last annex added and the whole clipped into a neat folder, the plan is obsolete. The contingency has declined in importance, or the circumstances have changed, and if you have to meet the contingency you will do so in an entirely different way.

Contingency planning is necessary, of course. The important thing you have at the end, though, is not the plan but the trained planners and the machinery of planning.

We planned hard, but even further from reality than before. Our real assets we now recognised were the planners and the machinery of planning; and the basic technique for landing a unit at short notice. These assets we developed. By the end of our time at sea we had reached a state where we could keep, for long periods, one company at ten minutes notice to leave the mess-decks – able, perhaps, to touch down at any Landing Site within range of the ship within one hour of the order reaching the ship.

This standard took time to achieve. We worked hard with HMS *Victorious* for nine days. We fitted in some straight military training to keep our standards up – shooting at balloons and cans thrown into the sea, weapon handling, keeping fit particularly. We had some rest and recreation: volley ball, deck hockey (a violent game) and films shown in the hangar every night.

At the end of nine days we were as fully trained as we could be without landing exercises. We had got used to the ship and the ship had got used to us. We were then told that we were to transfer to HMS *Albion*. Remarking that the Admiralty seemed to think that we wore out aircraft carriers, like boots, at the rate of one a week, we got ready to tranship.

The transfer took place in Mombassa on 9 February. HMS *Albion* (Captain C.D. Madden CBE, MVO, DSC) was a fully equipped Commando Ship with all modern conveniences. Inevitably many of our problems were eased. There was more space for the unit, proper mess-decks with bunks, proper storerooms and offices. There was a specially designed Assault Operations Room; special radio and a special internal broadcasting system. Life was easier, but we still had to go through the whole painful process again, more or less from scratch, setting up the planning teams and rehearsing the drills and procedures.

We reached our basic standards again and improved on them. We could not test them though. All our rehearsals ended with the men doubling over to the helicopters and away again. We would have to land somewhere if we were to test the machinery properly. Besides, we were worried about our military skills and our fitness. A unit cooped up in an aircraft carrier can lose its efficiency quickly, however hard it trains on board. We needed a proper landing exercise, with as much time ashore as possible.

We found a testing ground at Malindi, fifty miles north of Mombassa, and got permission to use it. The area was limited, but there was space to deploy the whole unit. We held two exercises there. Both followed the same pattern: we landed in two company Landing Sites simultaneously, then built up the rest of the unit in a third Landing Site, and deployed quickly, moving companies on foot and by helicopter. On the whole the exercises went well. One thing was abundantly clear. We were getting terribly unfit. We did what we could on board with PT and other exercises, but the only real answer was to get ashore and stay ashore for a few days. This we could never do, because of the short notice we were at.

Transferring stores from HMS *Victorious* to HMS *Albion*

HMS *Albion* had some Landing Craft (Assault) – flat–bottomed craft with ramps in the front, carrying thirty men or two Landrovers; so we had to learn new tricks. We trained in these and we did minor landing exercises. Captain Peter Brook and his Ferrets now came into their own. They had done excellent work at Dar-es-Salaam, but in HMS *Victorious* we had neglected them because we had no means of landing them. Peter discovered that his Ferrets could get into a LCA with ¾ inch to spare, so he experimented and landed them for training.

In between times we landed at Mombassa, and enjoyed ourselves the more after being cooped up in over-crowded ships. We were rested, refreshed, trained, and ready for any orders we might get.

We were ordered back to Aden.

We arrived off Aden on 26 February, five weeks after our embarkation. The men, stores and vehicles were landed by helicopter in a flurry of dust on the sandy parade ground just outside the camp. The GOC met us and came on board to look round the ship. We looked at the same old huts, the same sand and volcanic hills and oil storage tanks, and decided that it was beautiful and that it was nice to be home. We had enjoyed our sea-time and our visit to Tanganyika and the days and evenings ashore in Mombassa. Now we could settle down again.

Chapter 7

A Quiet Interlude

Aden hadn't changed much. In fact it hadn't changed at all, and March sped by like the wind just as every other month had done. There were the same conferences, seemingly about the same things; there were Visiting Firemen; there was Internal Security to prepare for. There was sport – we were late on the scene, but we won the Army Football Cup, by holding the final at home in front of our own crowd.

There was much to be done to tidy the administration after our series of rapid moves. The stores were in a muddle: all had to be checked, and repaired and replaced where necessary. Worst of all were the radio stores. Each radio had a long list of accessories that were mixed up or misplaced. Pat Howgill, whom I had never seen ruffled on exercise or operation, was ruffled. However he was called away for another job, and his place was taken by Jock Sim, a cheerful smiling Scotsman, who didn't find much to smile about for his first few weeks.

Above all there was the unit to train. We would have liked some rest. The companies had not had to work hard in the later days, and we had rested and relaxed during the fast voyage back to Aden. The whole unit had, however, been keyed to a state of immediate readiness for the best part of five weeks. It would have been nice to have let everyone relax for a week or two, doing only the essential administration. This could not be. Africa was still rumbling. There were signs of trouble in the Federation – while we had been away our own Rear Party had been called up from Aden to operate in the mountains near Dhala, carpenters, cooks and all. There were, as ever, question marks suspended over many parts of the Middle East. We were still reserve battalion, no less so in our camp in Little Aden than we had been when embarked in aircraft carriers. At any moment a code word could come, or a veiled message on the telephone, and we would start another riotous embarkation, or send the first company racing to the Khormaksar airfield.

We had no knowledge of what was to come. Tanganyika might have been an isolated incident in the long period of waiting and training that had begun after Kuwait and might stretch indefinitely into the future. Yet the Middle East in 1964 did not smell the same as it had done in 1963. Perhaps Tanganyika had made us acutely aware of how suddenly things could happen. Anyway most of us assumed that we would probably find ourselves on the move again soon.

I spoke to the whole unit and told them that we must train now and rest later, and told them why.

It may seem strange that a unit should need hard training immediately after a successful operation. They usually do. Operations provide, in a sense, the best training one can get and the only real test of the machinery. Yet something is always lost – precision; and sometimes flexibility of mind as well. Precision is lost because the actions taken are not those in the book but expedients, based on the book but adapted to the circumstances. If the operation goes well the expedients become a habit. If it does not, other and more hasty expedients are adopted. Untidiness creeps in everywhere – hurried shooting, clumsy weapon handling, strange tactics and untidy battle procedure, all because so much goes on without the close supervision given on training.

Something is always found out, too: faulty techniques. No CO can rest until he has put these mistakes right.

Tanganyika had not provided much of training value. We learnt about the helicopter assault, and we could turn our hand to it quickly again if need be. The land operations, however, had been far too brief and too simple, and had gone too well. We had seen the deployment drills work quickly and efficiently, and that helped to give substance to our training in these matters. There was nothing more – nothing, that is, except the enormous confidence that comes from a job well done. We were pleased with ourselves. But over-confidence is dangerous. There was only one cure for that – hard training. We trained.

We trained at the elementary skills of shooting and weapon handling, we trained at section tactics, we worked slowly towards a unit exercise. Inevitably we held an HQ exercise, five days after landing at Little Aden.

I wrote a new training directive, in which I coined the term manoeuvre – or rather resurrected it. 'Fire and movement' was the current phrase for minor tactics. It was a useful phrase; but it sometimes encourages men to fire at the wrong time, when all that was needed was a bit of craft. Besides, manoeuvre carried wider connotations – the analysis of ground, the careful choice of lines of approach even before contact had been made, the balance between speed on the one hand and safety on the other. The companies manoeuvred over hills, they manoeuvred in the heat of the day and they manoeuvred at night.

I also told the companies to get ready for operations in the mountains. The main thing was to get fit. We were painfully aware of our flabbiness after five weeks without hard exercise. I tried the scramble course a few times, gingerly at first, and then decided on a full-power trial, a timed run. I set off at a lumbering trot, and half way up the hill I passed Jock Sim and another officer, going rather slowly for young men – I did not know that they were limbering up for a run at dawn next morning. Honour decreed that they should accelerate. Honour decreed that I should not let them pass. By skilful use of my elbows I succeeded. I pounded along, they pounded behind me, and I got in first. I checked my time, found it was quite good, knocked a few seconds off for luck, and published it as the Slowest Acceptable Time. A lot of people went over the scramble course in their own time, some of them every day, and some remarkable times were produced.

HMS *Albion* had gone away, but she was due back again, and we began to prepare an exercise. The planning and reconnaissance was more or less completed when the exercise was cancelled at the last moment. I wanted another short unit exercise, to make sure that the whole machinery of the unit was running smoothly, so we knocked one together quickly. We chased some elusive 'dissidents', with light aircraft and Peter Hart and his Belvederes to help us, and finished with a day advance on to the hills behind Little Aden. Even with the kindest umpiring it was obvious that climbing hills by daylight against opposition was a mugs game, and we thought again about the night.

I renewed my attacks on the staff to get improvements made to the camp. By this time I was conditioned to the fact that little money could be spent on the place, because it would not be used much longer, and I had set my heart on one improvement only. I wanted to get a large and useless 'Quiet Room', behind the NAAFI, air-conditioned and converted into an English pub so that the Marines would have somewhere to drink in the summer time other than the simmering patio. It would have cost about £3,000. I bullied, I wheedled, I almost threatened. I dragged Visiting Firemen to see the place. I got much sympathy but no money. Such places were not allowed for in the official scales for Aden – nor, I muttered, were camps like mine. The Staff twisted the regulations as far as they could. Eventually the regulations broke in the right place and the plan was approved. Then came new and interminable delays – technical problems, procedures and so on. Almost my last act before leaving the unit was a plea that work on the place should start before I left. The room remained as it was, whitewashed, empty and silent, the quietest Quiet Room ever.

Chapter 8

The Radfan

April came and with it the first of the summer heat, intense and close, sapping the energy. The winter had not been cool, but pleasant enough when you did not have to work too hard, and with the cool evenings to look forward to. Now even the nights became hot. The climate was relentless, pursuing you everywhere except when you escaped into an air-conditioned room, and it hit you all the harder when you came out. We got used to it, and worked and trained hard, but it was less amusing.

I met Roy Watson, CO of 1st Battalion FRA, and heard much about the 'Nutcracker' operation in the Radfan, which he commanded. The operation had been a success, the tribes had sued for peace and the FRA had withdrawn. Then the trouble in Radfan flared again and Roy went back up country.

In late April I was visiting HQ FRA when a message came in to say that Roy Watson and John Monk (GSO2 of FRA) had been badly wounded and were being flown down by helicopter. Their Landrover had been blown up on a mine on the Dhala Road near the Radfan: John Monk had severe internal injuries and Roy, sitting in the front, had been wounded in the head and arm. I met the helicopter at Khormaksar. Roy was shaken, rugged as ever, and insisted on walking to the ambulance. John was in a bad way and managed no more than a slight grin and a half-raised hand in recognition. He died a few days later after a brave fight for his life. Roy later made a complete recovery.

A little before that I had been called into HQ Middle East and told that British troops were to operate with the FRA in the Radfan. 45 Commando was to be spearhead for the first advance. We had a fortnight to train, plan and get there.

'Radfan' is a loose term describing a geographical area of 300 square miles or more lying east of the Dhala Road just beyond where the road enters the mountains. There were two main entrances, such as they were. With the village of Thumier on the Dhala Road as jumping off point, the first was the Wadi Misra, a deep valley with a line of hills rising steeply 2,000 feet on either side, leading southwest towards the Jebel Radfan.

The other led up the Wadi Rabwa, through the Rabwa Pass into the Wadi Taim. The Wadi Taim was a broad and more or less flat basin three miles wide and nine miles long; the most fertile and most populated part of the Radfan. This in turn gave new entrances to the mountains to the south, particularly along the Bakri Ridge, rising steadily southwards to a point later known as Arnold's Spur, where the ground dropped suddenly into the Wadi Dhubsan.

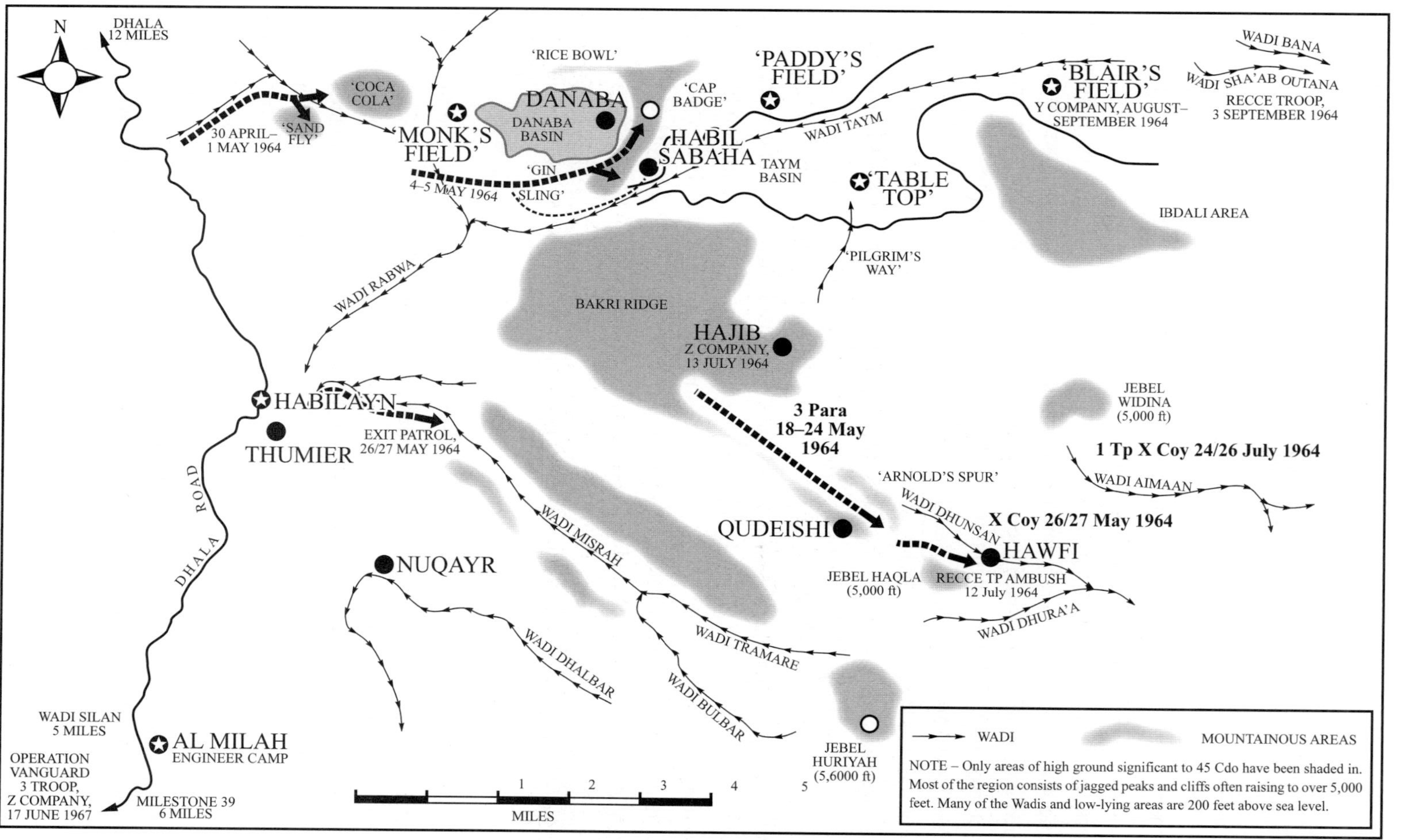

The Radfan, 1964–65

Arnold's Spur. Along the Bakri Ridge where it led down to Wadi Dhubsan.

The mountains were unpleasant; and it was all mountains, except in the Wadi Taim and the adjacent Danaba Basin. They were high, rugged, broken and confusing, usually with little vegetation except small patches of scrub, only bare rock, often crumbling, always hot to the touch. In many places there were steep cliffs, unclimbable, because of the way the rock crumbles, even to skilled climbers – and we had several in the unit. In places, where the rock had crumbled badly or split with the heat, there were slopes of scree or great chunks of rock fallen away; or, worse, seeming about to fall away. Apart from the wadi bottoms and the Bakri Ridge there were few tracks through the mountains; even fewer leading to the mountain tops; and these, through centuries of inter-tribal strife and mountain warfare, were well known and well defended.

There were many tribes in the Radfan, and no-one knew how big they were or where their boundaries lay. No-one had ever bothered to count; or rather no-one who wanted to count had been allowed in.

The Radfan tribes are a xenophobic lot. Every man had been brought up from boyhood with a rifle in his hands, and knew how to use it, and not infrequently did if a disagreement could not be settled or if there was other reasonable excuse. The arrival of the geish (army, whether British of RFA) was generally considered a reasonable excuse, an intrusion on the sovereignty of the area, and anyway good target practice.

When, later, we tried to assess the number of dissidents operating against us, we believed that there were many gradations – hard-core dissidents, trained outside the area and sent in to make trouble; men or groups with a grievance; men 'agin the government'; men instinctively reacting against intruders; and men out for the shooting.

They were fit, astonishingly fit, as men brought up in such mountains must be. They could run up and down the hills in a way that was exhausting to watch, and they could do it on remarkably little water. They were not cowards, and would stay and fight if there was a reasonable chance or if there was something worth fighting for.

Of their wider military ability there was much difference of opinion. My own opinion, based on talks with Roy Watson and others and confirmed by our experience throughout the campaign, was not a high one. They had always been fighters and had shown that they could fight well in circumstances. In recent years many Radfan tribesmen had gone to the Yemen to serve as mercenaries in the army there when money was short at home, and had returned with some military training and a new rifle. However they did not seem to like operating by night, and even used torches to find their way about. They were not, understandably, good at fighting co-ordinate battles. Their intelligence of our movements was far worse than it should have been. On the whole they did not shoot particularly straight. They would not fight close, by day or by night. And they did not make full use of the enormous advantages they had in operating on their own ground.

When they fought on their own terms and in their traditional way, however, they were formidable. They would take to the high ground, disappear behind a rock or into a small cave or a sangar (a loose term for a stone-built position), and shoot steadily at anyone below them: against soldiers toiling slowly up the high broken slopes in great heat, half-a-dozen men could hold up a brigade.

They had wonderful powers of observation, the eyesight of men who sat hour after hour, year after year, watching their own rugged countryside, noticing a stray goat or camel or the stranger coming too close to their fields. If their shooting was not all that it was said to be, they could spot the slightest target and plug away at it steadily.

They usually chose their ground well, they knew the best approaches to the high ground and had built good sangars – many of them built for private wars long before the British ever came, developed and improved until they were immune from gunfire and air attacks except by direct hits. Even their houses, with thick stone walls and built like forts, were sited well, often on the slopes, sometimes on pinnacles of rock, covering their fields and wells.

Thus, if you chose to fight them on their own terms and by day, and got caught in a wadi bottom or on the lower slopes of a hill under the steady fire of the tribesmen, there was not very much you could do about it.

A typical sangar

The conflict between the Radfani tribes and the Government goes back for generations, and much of it has hung on their right to extract toll on traffic along the Dhala road. In 1881 the Emir of Dhala imposed taxes on this traffic and denied the Radfan tribes their cut. They rose in rebellion, and an expedition had to be sent from Aden. In 1903 another expedition, which included British troops, sent because of raiding by a Radfan tribe, advanced deep into the Radfan. During this expedition a lot of trouble was caused by a single sniper; his position was heavily engaged by artillery fire, but within a few minutes of it ceasing he was firing again. As will be seen, Aden had not changed much.

The immediate cause of the trouble in 1964 was once again interference with traffic on the Dhala Road. The Arab troops of the Federal Regular Army had launched Operation 'Nutcracker' in late December 1963, and had secured the Rabwa Pass after some fighting. They had operated into the Danaba Basin, where they had run into trouble at Danaba itself, by fire from the towering hill later known as 'Cap Badge'. A column had advanced right along the Bakri Ridge to the southern point, and looked down into the Wadi Dhubsan (our own Reconnaissance Troop commander, Lieutenant Anthony Langdon, had accompanied them as a Forward Air Controller). By late February the tribes had come to terms, and the FRA withdrew.

In March the trouble had broken out again, this time more serious and more dangerous, an attempt to bring down the newly formed Arab Federation of South Arabia, by disrupting the economy and by inciting other parts of the Federation to revolt after the example of the Radfan. Propaganda had distorted the FRA withdrawal into a great military victory for the dissidents, and the Radfan was proclaimed as the first great front for the 'Liberation of the Occupied Yemen South'. Apart from the usual sniping and ambushes on the Dhala Road there were attacks on the Federal Guard posts. From these and from the FRA's first contacts it was apparent that the dissidents were more determined and better equipped. They were receiving money, ammunition and modern rifles; and there were believed to be 200 'hard-core' dissidents with military training, some of them in uniform.

Another view of Bakri Ridge, a vital piece of high ground

Significantly, whereas the tribes of the Radfan had usually quarrelled among themselves, they now appeared to be acting in concert – a potential of several thousand armed men. Significantly, the usual sources of intelligence were drying up – an ominous sign in a dissident area, showing that the dissidents had either won the loyalty of the tribes or had frightened them into submission. Perhaps it was a combination of loyalty and fear: loyalty, not to a new and dynamic leader, for there was no evidence that such a man had appeared, but to an 'arab cause', the idea that all the hardships of life in the mountains were due to the British, and that the Arab government of the Federation was merely a 'tool of the imperialists' – and the perennial and universal dream that if the existing powers were swept away a new age of freedom and happiness would arrive: fear, not only of the handful of hard-core dissidents and of the powerful tribes, but of what the future would hold for tribes who did not help in the 'liberation'. The British would soon be gone, so they were told, and after their departure the Federation would crumble before the new power. Anyway the British never came into the mountains, they no doubt believed that they could keep the FRA out – particularly after the great dissident 'victory' of January – and all around them was evidence of the growing strength and organisation of the dissidents. In so remote a place, far from immediate help by the geish, it would be a resolute man who could argue with the dissidents around him or risk the punishments that would be inflicted on his family.

This was the area into which we were to operate in the hottest month of the year – a big area, full of unpleasant hills and potentially unpleasant men, little known of the size and positions of the enemy, and not much known about the country itself.

We had several discussions about how we were to get into the Radfan, and in particular how to get on to the hilltops. The FRA had usually operated by day, trusting to the speed and agility of the Arab troops. The Commando was very fit, probably as fit as any British troops anywhere, but we could not keep up with the FRA in their fast daylight climbs. Against the tougher opposition now expected, even the FRA would be likely to find daylight climbing expensive.

A direct approach by helicopter was considered. Such tactics had been used successfully by the French in Algeria. The French, though, had had a very large and rather different area to operate over, large numbers of troops and many helicopters. The Radfan, though it seemed big enough to us, was relatively small, and there were villages everywhere. Above all, we could only count on four Belvederes serviceable at any one time. With so few helicopters available a few quick calculations showed that a helicopter assault would be too risky – we could never build up, in time, a big enough force to keep the enemy out of shooting distance of the Landing Site or the approach routes. The helicopters would have to go for the hill-tops, the Landing Sites were few and often difficult, the key hills perhaps occupied, and the steady stream of helicopters needed for the build up would provide fine target practice for the long-range shooting of the tribesmen.

I believed that the best chance lay in going through the hills by night, and climbing on to our objectives by night. It would be difficult, clambering over the broken unmapped ground during the hot nights; but the night would nullify the main advantages of the dissidents, their long-range shooting at climbing men from hidden positions; and so far they had shown no desire for night fighting, and they might be taken by surprise.

A special force was created for the operation, under Brigadier L. Hargroves, who normally commanded Aden Garrison. Allotted to the force were:

1st and 2nd Battalions FRA
45 Commando RM
B Coy of 3rd Bn Parachute Regiment (From Bahrain)
Coy of 1st Bn Royal Anglian Regiment
J Battery of 3rd Royal Horse Artillery (105mm guns, with a range of 9,000 yards)
Some tanks of the 16th/5th Royal Lancers
Armoured Cars of 4th Royal Tank Regiment
653 Light Aircraft Squadron.

It was a powerful force. You do not go to war to have a fair fight. You go to win, quick, and with as few casualties as possible. Even with such a force we did not underestimate our difficulties. It had a big area to cover, and against it was an enemy of unknown strength, perhaps several thousand men fighting on ground they knew well, very difficult ground at that, nullifying the effect of our technical superiority. The main part of our work would have to be done, as ever, by a few hundred men armed with rifles, moving on their flat feet.

Supporting this force, whose strength and composition changed from time to time, would be the RAF – Beverleys and Pembrokes to fly stores, Peter Hart and his Belvederes to carry men and stores in the forward area, Hunters for air strikes. I do not describe the work of the RAF much in the following pages. There was always an aircraft buzzing in the distance or close behind us.

Except in passing I do not describe the work of any part of the force except my own. 653 Light Aircraft Squadron of the Army Air Corps will appear often in the narrative. They were commanded by Lieutenant Colonel F Graham Bell, formerly of the Fleet Air Arm, a helicopter pilot of great experience, who could point out his helicopter in our Officer's Mess painting of 45 Commando's landing at Suez. His Beavers and Austers were around us every day, on reconnaissance or carrying officers on liaison visits. The newly acquired Scout helicopters, carrying three passengers, were used for almost everything – liaison, reconnaissance, casualties, troop lift, re-supply, even postal service. The Scouts would land almost anywhere, particularly if there was a casualty to be picked up: they would land on broken hill-sides, their spinning rotor blades within a few feet of the rocks, and 'Landing Sites' only a few feet square; they would fly in all weathers and they would fly under fire. Every Scout was hit by bullets during the Radfan campaign; and when they were hit they were taken back to Aden, patched up overnight, flight-tested at dawn, and back in the Radfan in the morning. They were a remarkable lot.

Another remarkable lot was 'A' Squadron, 22nd Special Air Service Regiment.

The whole of the ground force was to concentrate at Thumier, (see photo right) a village on the Dhala Road opposite the north end of the Radfan. There was a small airstrip there, and Thumier would be developed as the main base, with Force HQ, the administrative services and the stocks of water, fuel and ammunition.

Such intelligence as we had, suggested that the town of Danaba, where FRA had met trouble in January, was the centre of dissident activity in the north part of the Radfan. The Force Commander decided that his first step must be to secure the high ground surrounding the Danaba Basin.

The Base camp at Thumier

The key objective was the high feature nicknamed 'Cap Badge' between the Danaba Basin and the Wadi Taim, towering 1,500 feet above the flatter ground on either side, dominating the surrounding plains. It was a natural fort, its sides sheer in places, particularly to the north-west, and with only one climb that looked tolerably easy – the south-west, the furthest side from us.

On the north side of the Danaba Basin was a long line of high broken hills nicknamed 'Rice Bowl', stretching for two miles and virtually linking up with 'Cap Badge'. With both the 'Rice Bowl' and 'Cap Badge' in our hands we could dominate Danaba and the Danaba Basin and force the tribes to either withdraw or come to terms

The Force Commander decided to hold the dissident attention by an attack towards the Rabwa Pass by armour, FRA and a company of Royal Anglians; to drop B Company into the Wadi Taim by parachute, to secure 'Cap Badge'; and to send 45 Commando through the hills north of Rabwa Pass to secure 'Rice Bowl'. B Company was to come under my command after dropping.

This high feature was nicknamed 'Cap Badge'

One of the ideas underlying this plan was the hope that the dissidents would attack us on ground of our own choosing. The Radfan tribes had never shown much inclination to fight on ground of anyone's choosing except their own, and it was doubtful if they would commit the folly of a daylight attack uphill against automatic weapons. Nevertheless there was always the chance that they would not at first realise the British troops were there and in strength, and they might expose themselves to heavy casualties before they learnt better. Even if they did not attack we would be no worse off. From these hills we could dominate the Danaba Basin and the Wadi Taim, and the Radfan would be wide open for whatever plan we chose to make.

Much of the force would be tied to securing the base at Thumier and protecting the Dhala Road. The armour could not get into the Wadi Taim yet, and the guns could not yet get into position to cover all sides of 'Cap Badge'. As ever, the main risks would be born by infantrymen – the 120 men of B Company on their own in the Wadi Taim, and the 250 men of the Commando trying to link up with them. Against them would be an unknown number of tribesmen fighting on their own ground. Hence there was a need for the diversion to the Rabwa Pass to be maintained for as long as possible. With these odds we were not worried about the outcome in a straight fight. Our one fear was that part of the force might be caught in daylight in low ground deep in the Radfan, with tribesmen gathering in the hills above them.

In the initial plan – though not as things developed – our task was a subsidiary one, to get into position to support B Company at the key objective and to secure the north side of the Danaba Basin. Nevertheless we had to get through the hills.

Planning was difficult – as the main map at that time was what was known as 'chocolate and custard', with any rocky excrescence above the 'custard' of the plains shown in 'chocolate'. This was fine as far as it went; but as an excrescence might be anything from fifty to 2,000 feet high the maps did not help in detailed planning. Air photographs were taken, and with the help of these, supplemented by frequent (but discreet and high) flights over the ground in light aircraft, we were able to get a tolerable idea of the ground.

Our objective, 'Rice Bowl', would be appalling going at night, broken and shapeless as it was. However I was satisfied that, provided we could get on to the west end of it before first light, we could fight our way along it against opposition. The real problem was getting there.

The country north of the Rabwa Pass was broken, with quite high hills intersected with deep wadis. Six miles north of Thumier a nameless wadi wound easily (we thought) in the right direction; then after a mile across country we could get into the Wadi Boran, and follow its deep gorge between two high features known as 'Sand Fly' and 'Coca Cola', which would take us into the Danaba Basin and to within easy striking distance of 'Rice Bowl'. Because of security I was only allowed a half-hour recce of the approach from ground level, and could only fly over it, discreetly high, a couple of times. I was satisfied that we could get through; and I left my Recce Troop commander, Lieutenant Langdon, to make a more detailed study from the air and from air photographs and to prepare a map of the route, and eventually to lead us through as far as the Wadi Boran.

Of the tribes and the enemy here we knew little. Our route lay somewhere near the border between the northern Radfan tribes and the Halmain. The Halmain tribes were believed to be friendly, but you could not be sure with these large tribes how a particular section would react. Anyway dissidents had operated against the Dhala Road near this point. The FRA picquetting the Dhala Road had reported seeing dissident scouts on some of the hilltops, and there had been some exchanges of fire, but the approach did not appear to be strongly held. There was no reason why it should be. There were six miles of hill to penetrate on this route, the dissident scouts could spot any movement easily, and a few men could delay an advance for several hours until reinforcements came. We hoped they would not guess that we intended to move by night; anyway they could not cover every night route.

Back at Little Aden the unit was preparing, moving at night over the scramble course and the other hills around. Every company made night marches, carrying their full scale of equipment, ammunition and water.

Ammunition was a big problem. We were going to be outside the range of our guns, so we decided to man-pack our mortars and Vickers Machine Guns, which meant extra ammunition for every man to carry. We had reservations about the mortars, as their value against the dissidents in good sangars would be negligible; but they might be the only heavy support we would get for much of the time. About the Vickers we had no doubts at all: an ancient weapon, in service for over fifty years, its sustained and accurate firing at long range would be of tremendous value – provided we could carry the ammunition.

Commando HQ would also have to be man-packed, which was not easy with the heavy wireless sets and batteries. We worked out a small HQ of sixteen men, with only the essential officers, wireless operators and the men to carry the spare sets and batteries.

The main problem was going to be water. The Radfan was hot. At that time of year there was little water in the hills except in the wells and reservoirs near the villages and the occasional, very occasional small pools. There would be none on the hilltops. We estimated that men would normally drink a gallon and a half a day with reasonable exertion; with the kind of exertion we were going to have they would need two gallons or more – twenty pounds per man in addition to his weapon and equipment and the extra ammunition he would have to carry. The usual answer to this problem was to use part of the unit as porters, lightly equipped so that they could carry great loads, and probably returning to base after dropping off their loads. This was no use to us. The porters would have to accompany us right on to 'Rice Bowl'; by the time they got there it would be daylight, and they would be stuck there all day with the rest of us, drinking water.

We would have to be our own porters. We would carry only three water bottles per man (¾ gallon). With this I believed we could last through the night march and until mid-day, by which time the re-supply should arrive by helicopter. If it did not, we would have to last out longer.

These were big loads for every man to carry, and we cut out every ounce that was not essential. Even washing gear was cut to a flannel and a toothbrush. There would be no water for washing and shaving until the water re-supply was generous, and our packs could come up then.

B Company 3rd Parachute Battalion arrived in Aden. Hearing that they were going to be put into the transit camp I arranged for them to come and live with us. The training was better there, and we wanted to get to know them. They arrived, commanded by Major Peter Walter, MBE, MC; they were a fine company, and they settled in quickly and started hard training in the hills.

I finally moved up to Thumier in late April with a small planning team; followed later by the company commanders. We flew high above the Radfan in Beavers and

Scouts, studied the ground we would have to walk over, and didn't like it much. In fact we did not like the Radfan at all at that stage, an unknown medium and a little alarming. Slowly the mass of tumbling hills began to take on a pattern: a revolting hill, barely distinguishable from the revolting hills around it, earned a nickname and was seen to have a certain shape – never attractive, but there were clearly routes to the top. Slowly the unknown became familiar and lost its power. A plan began to form in my mind. I gave each company commander a definite area to study and reconnoitre, and retired to a hot tent, surrounded by iced drinks and a growing pile of cigarette ends, to make my plan.

I had been told that I could only take two companies to 'Rice Bowl', because of the problem of re-supply – the maximum size of the force for penetration could be fairly accurately calculated by the amount of water that could be carried by the helicopters.

Lt Col Paddy Stevens with Brig Chandos Blacker on 'Cap Badge', May 1964

I allotted X and Y Companies to 'Rice Bowl'. However I was worried about the Boran gorge. It was flanked by two high features, 'Sand Fly' to the west and 'Coca Cola' to the east. If we ran into trouble passing through the gorge it would be nice to have someone on the high ground, even at night. 'Coca Cola' was the higher of the two; but it lay back a bit from the gorge; and anyway it would be a difficult climb at night, its sides almost sheer in places on our nearest approach. 'Sand Fly' was easier.

Besides, 'Sand Fly' had a lower ledge, which provided not only command over the gorge but an alternative route if we were held up in the gorge itself – the company there would either clear and mark the new route while we were back-tracking, or make a dash for 'Rice Bowl' themselves. Holding 'Sand Fly' would not only give us security but a more flexible plan, much needed with so little knowledge about the ground and the enemy.

I got permission to deploy my third company. They would have a shorter march, and if helicopters were not available to re-supply them it would not be difficult to effect a ground re-supply. I allotted Z Company to secure 'Sand Fly'. They were to remain there after we had passed, to cover a route for the helicopter re-supply of 'Rice Bowl'.

A RAF Beverley landing at Thumier airfield

We carried out our final reconnaissance in a Beaver. Peter Walter, though he was not under my command yet, came with us, and then went back to Aden to prepare for his parachute drop.

The unit joined me at Thumier late on 29 April, with just twenty-four hours to go. We had left our green berets behind, as we did not want the dissidents to know that Commandos were being used – in our floppy desert hats we could be mistaken for other British troops who normally supported the FRA at Thumier. I gave my final orders, some key men flew on reconnaissance, and all officers and NCOs went in small groups to some hills close around Thumier, from which they could just see the tops of the distant hills they would have to climb.

Chapter 9

'Cap Badge'

On the afternoon of the 30 April we drove up the Dhala Road, debussed under cover and lay up in some scrub near our start point. We had a final meal, topped ourselves up with water, and waited. There was some shooting from in front of the picquet lines at two Scouts that passed low overhead, then all was quiet. We did not know it at the time but the Scouts were carrying the pathfinders of 22nd SAS, who were to have marked the Dropping Zones: both helicopters were hit and were returning to base. We did not know it but another party of 10 men of the SAS were fighting for their lives near the Rabwa Pass, cut off by 200 tribesmen: they shot their way out at dusk, leaving two dead behind. For us, all was quiet. As the light began to fade we set off along the wadi led by Lieutenant Langdon and the navigating party.

X Company (Mike Banks) were leading, followed by Tac HQ, then Y Company (Gavin Hamilton-Meikle) with Z Company (David Langley) bringing up the rear. We moved in single file, a long snake of 400 men walking steadily up the wadi bed, quickly at first to make as much ground as we could while the light remained, then ever more slowly. Soon it was pitch dark, the moon still down and the steep hills each side of us excluding much of the light from the sky. We could see only a few yards, and what had seemed from the air to be an easy route now became full of difficulties – boulders in the wadi bed, side wadis leading temptingly away at a point where the main wadi disappeared through the added darkness of boulders and scrub.

We had memorised Langdon's sketch map, and by counting the paces and checking the turns in the wadi we knew roughly where we were; even so there were moments of doubt, when we checked our compasses and seemed to be moving far off course. Just as I began to feel that we were lost the navigating party would report over the radio that they had reached a Report Line (the occasional obvious bend or wadi junction).

The column closed up whenever the front stopped at an obstacle or to check direction; then suddenly opened out alarmingly as the leading troops set off again at what seemed to be a fast lope. This 'telescoping' continued. Three times the column broke in the darkness and we had to halt until contact was made again. Three times it was halted as reports came in or Arabs seen or heard near the column – once two men were reported crossing the skyline near Tac HQ. The navigating party reported finding fresh prints of sandals, leading away from us, in a patch of soft light sand.

David Langley reached his mark and broke off towards 'Sand Fly'. X Company encouragingly reported 'Puddle Corner', over half way to the Boran, a place where there had seemed to be two small pools in the wadi bed. Then the column stopped, and remained stopped for what seemed an hour in the quietness of the night.

I got on to Mike Banks by radio with the usual question 'What is the delay?' Mike said they were trying to find their way round one of the puddles. I asked how deep it was. Long pause, then the answer came back 'About two foot six'. 'Well, go through it you bloody idiot'. Mike muttered something incomprehensible, followed by 'Out'; and another long pause. Then the report came that they were traversing round the puddle, and the column began to move slowly. Traversing? These bloody mountaineers had to do fancy tricks rather than get their feet wet. I fumed, and slouched on with the column. We came to 'Puddle Corner': the water was certainly not deep, but there was a four foot drop before you reached the water, and two Marines were still being hauled out.

We traversed. The wadi side was vertical, and there was an overhang in one place so that men with heavy loads on their backs could not get past. I got over first, threw off my kit, braced myself into a corner, pulled HQ past the overhang one by one, and regained my place, feeling pleased. I was just in time to see the tail of Y Company go by. Forewarned by Mike's report, Gavin had reconnoitred higher up the side of the wadi and found a way round. I halted the column, HQ gained its rightful place and dignity, and we moved on again.

Shortly before midnight we had our first view of 'Coca Cola', a black outline on the night sky; and beyond it, blessed sight, the first glimmer of the moon. We were a bit behind schedule, but the ground had levelled off and we were moving fast; what's more, we knew for sure at last that Langdon and the navigating party were leading us right on target. We could make up time now, with the moon rising.

Parts of a message from the Force Commander had come through earlier, but it had been distorted, and all we had got was the name 'Coca Cola'. Now, on higher ground, we stopped and got the complete message. The parachute drop by B Company had been cancelled. We were on our own. We were to forget about 'Rice Bowl' and go firm on 'Sand Fly' and 'Coca Cola'.

I sat down to think that one out.

I was not worried about the dissidents, because I felt that any picquets they had out had been left far behind. I was worried about the ground. David Langley and Z Company were already up on 'Sand Fly', so that was no trouble. We had glanced at 'Coca Cola' on the air photographs and noted that the side nearest us was extremely difficult in places, but had not made a detailed study of the routes up it. It was no good looking at 'Coca Cola' now as it was just a black cardboard shape outlined against the first light of the moon The maps were as much use as a map of the London Underground. We peered at the air photographs by the light of shaded torches under a hastily rigged screen: that told us little except that it was a nasty climb: we knew that already. There was nothing for it but to walk straight at 'Coca Cola' and hope for the best.

It was now up to Mike Banks, for the navigating party had reached the end of its route. Anyway Mike was a mountaineer, and should be pleased at the original prospect of a 1,500-foot difficult climb unreconnoitred and in the dark. I told him, he muttered, and off we set again.

We were on level ground, and the going was now fast. There is a wonderful difference, too, when you can see the place you are heading for: but it can be deceptive. We descended 200 feet down a steep slope into a wadi, crossed the wadi quickly and climbed steadily the far side. Presumably this was the Boran. Then we climbed down again into another wadi. Presumably this was the Boran too, split into two at this place. We climbed, then descended yet again, this time on to flat ground. Looking at the ground ahead and around us told us little: there could have been a motorable track nearby for all we knew. We could see nothing. We could only plunge on.

At last the ground began to rise steeply, then more steeply still, until the top of 'Coca Cola' disappeared and we could see nothing but the dark line of cliffs above us. Still we climbed, with occasional halts as Mike searched for a better route. The pace and the heat and the need to conserve water were beginning to tell, particularly on the men carrying wireless sets and support weapons, but the column kept well together now. The moon was higher, but we were still in deep shadow.

The column stopped again, for too long it seemed. First light was less than two hours away; if there were dissidents on top and we did not get there before dawn we might have a harassing day. I told Mike to get moving. He said he was going as fast as he could and he didn't think anyone could go faster and if I had anyone in mind Mike would be delighted to meet him. I went forward to see what was wrong. By the time I got there Mike has just returned from fixing a rope up a particularly nasty cliff. We hauled ourselves up one by one. When I got to the top I found the rope secured, if that was the word, to a flimsy dehydrated bush. Mike said he'd hoped no one would notice.

After that the climb suddenly became easier. Mike reported that his leading troop had reached level ground. I told him to push on as fast as he could to the far end – the hilltop was a mile long – told Gavin to secure the near end, and we trundled over the rough ground in the footsteps of the fast receding men of X Company. At 0400 hours, an hour before dawn, I reported to Force HQ that 'Coca Cola' was ours.

Dawn found us looking out over the Danaba Basin and into the back of the Rabwa Pass from this high and commanding hill, with Z Company a mile away to our right. 'Cap Badge' was still far in front of us; but we had outflanked the Rabwa Pass and held a clear path leading into the Radfan. Not a shot had been fired.

We did not meditate much, as we were thirsty. I still had a bottle and a half left, and that was about the average. We could have survived the day, even after that hard and unexpected climb; but we didn't have to. Soon after dawn Peter Hart's Belvederes appeared, the most beautiful aeroplanes in the world with the silvery cans of water slung beneath them in nets. We added to the colour of the golden morning by throwing pink and blue smoke grenades to bring in the helicopters; and as the first cans were landed and issued we drank the rest of our water.

The sun came up and it was very hot. There was no shade of any kind except what we had brought with us – small rolls of hessian, for shade by day and for warmth in case of a windy night. I had no hessian, but a copy of the 'Times' had been sent up to me, which proved adequate.

Our packs never arrived. There was not enough air lift to spare, and the high winds on the narrow summit of 'Coca Cola' made it unwise to use the helicopters on any but essential trips. Anyway the packs were not vital, and we did not doubt that we would soon be walking again.

We spent three days on 'Coca Cola' and 'Sand Fly', cooked by the sun each day, a little chilled at night. During that time the Force Commander gave me my next task, to take 'Cap Badge'.

We had played our surprise card of night infiltration, so we had new difficulties. 'Cap Badge' was a most commanding feature, which would give us control over the whole of the Wadi Taim and the choice of several routes on to the Bakri Ridge. If this was obvious to us it must be obvious to the dissidents, and I expected to have to fight for 'Cap Badge'. With a steep climb up narrow and obvious approaches it was not going to be easy.

I decided that I must have two simultaneous bites at it. We would need luck, and if luck ran against us on one route it might run with us on the other. One company would cut straight across the Danaba Basin to the south-west approach to 'Cap Badge': a relatively short route, only 5½ miles from our start point in the Wadi Boran, but a difficult climb up a narrow approach – and the most obvious approach being the most direct.

There was no point in concentrating more than one company on this approach. A dozen dissidents could stop two companies on this narrow approach as easily as they could stop one. I needed a second string to my bow. The west and south routes I ruled out because of the high cliffs, the north because it would mean passing Danaba, a known dissident centre. That left only the south-east approach, two miles longer, but much of it on the fast, flat going of the Wadi Taim, and with an easier climb at the end and a broader final approach. It was a long march; but it was practicable, given luck.

Of course we might have no luck at all and bump into dissidents in strength on both routes, in which case we would be caught at first light with both companies in the low ground below 'Cap Badge'. I decided to use the third company to take 'Gin Sling', a high feature one mile south of 'Cap Badge'. This was another unpleasant climb at night, but slightly less so than 'Cap Badge', and it had enough variety in the approaches to give us a good chance of fighting our way to the top if we met trouble. If either or both the other companies failed to get on top of 'Cap Badge' they could at least be partly protected by 'Gin Sling'. If the worst came to the worst and a company was caught in the low ground, it should kick its way into a village and stay there under the protection of the strong walls until we could support it.

B Company had now arrived at Thumier and was placed under my command for the operation. I gave them the most difficult task, the long march to the southeast approach: they were fresh and they had studied the approach. X and Y, who were with me on 'Coca Cola', could study the direct approach as best they could through binoculars at four miles range. Mike Banks was to go for 'Cap Badge', Gavin for 'Gin Sling'. Tac HQ would go on to 'Gin Sling'. We would be relieved on 'Coca Cola' and 'Sand Fly' by the Royal Anglians, who had now arrived at Thumier, so Z Company would be available as a reserve to be flown forward if needed.

The diversionary attack on the Rabwa Pass was called off, but the attention of the dissidents was maintained there by some remarkable work by the SAS infiltrating among them. Z Company added to the deception by ranging mortars and Vickers in that direction and by sending patrols, as though we were now planning a flank attack on Rabwa Pass.

On 4 May we were relieved by the Royal Anglians and we moved down the west side of 'Coca Cola' into the Wadi Boran, where we had a meal and formed up. B Company joined us there.

It was then that minor errors began to accumulate in a way that had an important effect later. I had allowed forty-five minutes to get down from 'Coca Cola' into the Boran; an apparently generous estimate based on patrol reports: it took well over an hour. X and Y Companies, after their hard march and three days in the sun and no shade, were more tired than I expected. The re-supply was 500 yards back from the RV arranged; which gave us an extra 1,000 yards to walk in all. Most serious, I had placed B Company at the back of the column and not at the front. I had done this because X and Y could study and reconnoitre the first part of the route from 'Coca Cola' and could therefore be expected to make faster going over the first stretch. It seemed a good idea at the time.

I had allowed plenty of slack in the timings; but these accumulating errors took up the slack, and we were well over half an hour late starting. This meant that instead of reaching the far end of the Boran just after dusk, we were still stumbling through it after dark, slowly in pitch-blackness between the walls of the gorge. We were nearly two hours late leaving the Boran.

Even so there was still time, provided we had luck. Once out of the Boran the going was fast across the Danaba Basin. B Company broke off on their separate route and disappeared into the darkness. Y Company's route-finding was excellent, and they led us accurately along the tracks and wadis and across open fields to the dispersal point. X Company made for 'Cap Badge', and Y Company turned south for 'Gin Sling' with HQ behind them.

We made a wide detour to avoid a village, then began the climb. It was not a particularly high hill, a little over 1,000 feet, but like most in the Radfan it was deceptively difficult, especially for climbing at night. We were more tired than we had been on our first night march. Both Gavin and his second-in-command Ted Goddard were trained climbers and kept steadily on. It was not the technique of climbing that counted but the fact that they could more quickly assess the profitable and unprofitable routes. We had a couple of dead ends and had to climb down again, but about two hours before first light the climb became steadier, the ground less broken, and we were obviously on the final ascent.

X Company also made good progress. They had anxious moments skirting a village. The dogs barked, but no alarm was given, and they pushed on up the slope. There were difficult patches, long delays when they met steep cliffs that had not been visible from the viewpoint on 'Coca Cola'. A final steep climb, clambering over high boulders and they were at the top, with only the tall pinnacle at the east end of 'Cap Badge' still to climb.

I reached a point about 200 feet from the summit of 'Gin Sling', where the ground had levelled off and there appeared to be routes leading round. Gavin had stopped there and was deploying his three troops to search and clear the crags around us. I move HQ 100 yards further east, to a point from which we could see 'Cap Badge' more easily, and stopped there. The radio operators were exhausted and had drunk more water than the last time. We stopped, and with the first glimmer of light in the east I called for radio reports from the companies.

Gavin reported the top of 'Gin Sling' clear of enemy. Mike reported that his leading troop was on the summit of 'Cap Badge', and he was now deploying his troops to search the feature and cover all the approaches on to it. There were strongly built sangars on the feature, and some of them were very much 'lived in', but there was no sign of any enemy. Both X and Y Companies reported flickering lights moving on the lower slopes behind them but could give no explanation. I discounted the reports.

B Company had been out of radio touch for some time, screened behind the hills. They had reported being level with 'Gin Sling' over an hour ago, and should make the lower slopes of 'Cap Badge' well before first light. I was satisfied. Incredibly, we had got 'Cap Badge' without a shot being fired.

As dawn came, scattered firing broke out from 'Cap Badge'. X Company reported that they were engaging dissidents who had evidently followed them up the slope. The firing continued, became heavy for a while, then died away as the dissidents realised that the high ground was strongly held. Evidently the dissidents had lived in their villages at night and moved up to their key positions at dawn. They were an hour too late.

At the same time, heavy firing broke out to our east, in the low ground below 'Cap Badge'. B Company were in action.

The luck had not run for B Company. After breaking away from the column outside the Wadi Boran they had had to move fast to make up time. They had had a tricky climb down the escarpment into the Wadi Taim, they had slightly lost direction a couple of times, and with the fast pace they had two cases of heat exhaustion. Peter Walter had left his rear platoon to bring these casualties along, and had then pushed on fast with the rest. Then, level with 'Gin Sling', the luck had run right out. They had twice seen parties of dissidents moving across the Wadi Taim with flickering torches, and had had to lie low until they had passed. This put them far behind schedule.

Dawn found them in the worst possible place, away from the protection of 'Gin Sling' and moving across the open ground towards the southeast slopes of 'Cap Badge'. Peter Walter, out of radio contact and not knowing that we were on both features, had rightly decided that his proper job was to push on hard towards the key objective. If he had to take cover, the nearest village lay half a mile in front of him Habil Sabaha, later called 'Pegasus Village'.

'Pegasus Village' with 'Cap Badge' in the background

At daybreak one of his platoons came under fire from dissidents on their left, in positions varying from one to four hundred yards away. The paratroopers immediately launched a violent attack, and the dissidents fled, leaving two casualties. The firing became more general. Peter himself, well forward with his leading platoons, led a quick attack against two strong, fort-like buildings lying right at the foot of 'Cap Badge'. The dissidents fled. The main fighting was still on the left, and Peter sent another platoon to attack a group of buildings there. They went in under heavy supporting fire and drove the dissidents out, killing several more of them.

Up to now it had been fine going. B Company had hit the dissidents hard, and now held strong houses in commanding positions. There was a lull in the fighting, and Peter began to re-organise his Company.

At this moment the luck ran against them again. Several of the dissidents had escaped into the hills immediately below 'Cap Badge'. Beaten on the flat ground they reverted to their traditional form of warfare. From their hidden sangars they began firing steadily at anything they could see.

Several men of B Company were wounded. Peter immediately ordered his rear platoon to get into the village of Habil Sabaha. They attacked and went in under cover of smoke grenades, led by the second-in-command Captain Jewkes. Soon after that one of the sergeants was hit and badly wounded out in the open. Jewkes went to him and was administering morphia when he too was shot. He died almost immediately. A young paratrooper, Lance Corporal Bruton, who had already led a gallant section attack, took over the group of wounded men here, got them into the best cover he could and controlled the fire of the men around him. Soon, as the sun began to get hot, he carried them across open ground into a building, with the help of another man.

During all this time B Company were fighting on their own. When the heavy firing began at first light I found my view blocked by a low hill. We moved forward on to this, found that there was yet another hill in front of us, and came under scattered fire from below us to the north. This firing was soon stopped, but HQ was out on its own, and 'Gin Sling' was a big feature. I ordered Gavin to send some of his troops to cover us. It took time over the broken hills, but they got into position on the high ground and on a flat shelf over-looking Habil Sabaha.

I had got Peter's first report, laconic and assured, but there was little we could do to help in the confusing battle raging below us until we knew where everyone was. Peter now gave me his positions, and I saw the rear platoons going into Habil Sabaha under cover of smoke.

There was still little we could do. B Company was out of artillery range and the position was too confused to use strike aircraft. X Company had peered into the haze below them on 'Cap Badge' and fired twice at groups of dissidents, but had stopped again for fear of hitting the paratroopers. Mike had his Vickers guns on top of 'Cap Badge', but by the time it was clear enough for him to see, the dissidents had disappeared into caves and sangars in the hillside 1,000 feet below him down an almost vertical cliff: he could neither see them nor shoot in their direction if he could have seen them. On 'Gin Sling' Gavin had a mortar ready as well as his Vickers, and waited for targets, but none came.

Peter reported all of his company safe inside buildings, and said laconically that they were 'quite happy here'. The action had quietened down and he was systematically locating and engaging the snipers. The main part of the action lasted little over an hour. B Company had so far had one killed and ten wounded, but were now completely under cover. We were secure on both 'Gin Sling' and 'Cap Badge', and the timid attempt by the dissidents to get back on to 'Cap Badge' had been beaten off – there had been sharp and accurate firing, I learnt later, with bullets hitting the rocks around the heads of X Company, but no casualties, and none confirmed to the dissidents.

All was secure. Most of the dissidents had disappeared. The main problem was extricating B Company, and, more important, getting the casualties out. Though the snipers in the hillside were fairly quiet now under the accurate fire of B Company, I had no doubt that they would open up again if they saw a good target: a company loaded with wounded would soon have more wounded to carry. It would need a whole company moving down from 'Cap Badge' to clear the broad and broken slopes below.

Though no more dissidents had shown an interest in 'Cap Badge' I was not prepared to send X Company down, or even part of it. 'Cap Badge' was a big feature, and it was what we were there to get and hold. I ordered B Company to remain in the village, and asked Force HQ to fly Z Company forward from 'Sand Fly' to 'Cap Badge'.

It was a long morning for B Company, most of all for the wounded, some of them badly hurt, in the hot Arab houses. Peter systematically located some of the snipers and dealt with them with his own fire and with air strikes. The Hunters came in low and accurately, and scored at least one direct hit on a building containing a sniper. Two Beavers flew low over the village and dropped water and ammunition by parachute, the firing increasing suddenly as they flew. Another paratrooper was killed collecting the air drop.

Then the sniping stopped altogether, partly because of B Company's fire and the air strikes, partly no doubt because the dissidents on the hillside now knew that we were above and around them. There were delays in the air lift of Z Company, but eventually David Langley and his leading troops were moving down the slopes, spreading out to cover the possible sniper positions. They made contact with B Company and covered the high ground immediately above them. A Belvedere landed, and there were long and anxious moments as the wounded were loaded. Then it swung away, and B Company climbed steadily up the slope to the top of 'Cap Badge'.

Chapter 10

The Deep Valleys

We spent three more days on Cap Badge. Aircraft flew over the Wadi Taim and the Danaba Basin dropping leaflets ordering the tribes to leave their valleys. The tribes left. We sent patrols down into the villages around, including Habil Sabaha, and found them deserted. On 8 May I sent B Company down into Habil Sabaha again for a last search. On 9 May we were relieved by the Royal Anglians and returned to Little Aden.

By then the dissidents had left the Rabwa Pass. The capture of Cap Badge had put us in their rear, with access to the long slope of the Bakri Ridge. The tribes on whose support the hard-core dissidents depended had gone; and they went too, with the tribes or by night, eastwards or into the high mountains to the south. The Radfan was wide open.

In Little Aden I spoke to the whole unit, including B Company, and described the operation. Each man had played his part, in the re-supply at Thumier, in the marches and fighting or in the communications. They should now know how the parts had fitted together. I then called Peter Walter out to give an account of B Company's action. They had fought a fine battle and killed a number of dissidents, and I wanted to hear the story first hand and, as it were, hot. Peter was as laconic as ever, and the account was the more impressive for the simple way he gave it.

B Company left us to return to Bahrain. We had a short rest and began to train for the next operation, which we knew would come soon.

B Company's casualties were on my conscience. You can never do anything if you are not prepared to risk casualties; but it is unpleasant when they come, and I wondered whether in this case they had been unavoidable. I had committed the cardinal error of mountain warfare of allowing one of my companies to be caught in low ground in daylight. Thinking again of Cap Badge I could find no better plan. It would have been no good concentrating on X Company's route: a few resolute dissidents there could have stopped two companies – or more for that matter – as easily as one. The march for B Company had not been too long and the final climb a relatively easy one. The truth was that we had been far too slow off the mark, which left B Company's timings so fine that they had no margin for the ordinary chances of war. Thereafter the luck had run against B Company. It could as easily have run against X Company. I had learnt that everything in the Radfan took longer than expected.

I mention luck many times. It is not the blind chance of the toss of the coin. In war there are too many unknown factors to permit mathematical certainty in a plan. There are the chances of weather, oddities in the ground, which you have not seen properly because the enemy has not permitted you to walk over it; errors and flashes of genius by the enemy; the same on your own side, their consequences sometimes negligible, sometimes crucial. A good plan is resilient enough to absorb the normal chances of war. In the plan for Cap Badge both X and B Companies needed luck: success as a whole – one company on Cap Badge – needed just half that little luck. When we left the Boran nearly two hours late B Company needed all the luck in the world. They did not get it.

If we had had any doubts about the effectiveness of the dissidents firing from their sangars into low ground we had none now. There were many sangars on Cap Badge, and they were well made indeed. One of them, twenty yards long and with only three small holes in it, I walked pass several times without noticing: at 200 yards it was impossible to see against the broken rocks and shadows of the hillside.

Later I was astonished to hear it said that 'fire and movement' was the fundamental principle of operations in the mountains. I could never agree. Fire and movement was fine, if you were more or less level with the dissidents or above them. It was not easy and it was always risky moving across the difficult hills; but it was practicable with our automatics and our air and gunfire support against the rifles and few light machine guns of the dissidents. The main problem, though, was how to get up to their level. Fire support was of little use, as you could not spot the enemy; and slow movement, uphill against hidden snipers, was expensive. For me the fundamental principle, from first to last, was surprise. This was in fact the principle that everyone exploited, usually by getting on to the high ground by night. Because it always worked it was taken for granted.

We did not have long to reflect, as we were soon up in the Radfan, on what was for most of us a dull and abortive visit. On 19 May we relieved the Royal Anglians in the Wadi Taim. the operations were now commanded by Brigadier C.H. Blacker, OBE, MC.

The dissidents had left the Wadi Taim. Understandably they were not prepared to fight on level ground against superior firepower. Our job was to keep them out, and to search the villages for guns, ammunition and secret food stores. It was dull, but we were only there for five days, while preparing ourselves for the next operation. We used much of the time for night training and field firing exercises in the empty valley. I took Commando HQ out for a night march – a strange exercise indeed, with bullets in our guns and knowing that any contact made meant immediate shooting. We carried out our drills for movement and control and changing formation more meticulously than we had ever done.

On the evening of 22 May some dissidents fired at very long range against our forward position. It was a tiresome interruption to our training. We set up patrols and I ordered that there was to be no firing back except at point blank range, and we hoped that next night they would come closer. They never came. On 25 May we were sent back to Thumier, except for X Company, who were flown on to the Bakri Ridge to join 3rd Bn Parachute Regiment.

There were dissident tribes in the high mountains to the south, and they too had to be dealt with. There were two main approaches leading into these mountains, the Bakri Ridge and the Wadi Misra.

A view of the Wadi Taim

It had been decided to advance up both routes, to keep the dissidents guessing. Using the helicopters for re-supply the logistic effort, and so the main thrust, could be switched from one axis to the other. To keep the impetus going a new unit had been brought into the Radfan, 3rd Bn Parachute Regiment. They had only two companies, the rest of the unit being back in Bahrain.

The Battalion had arrived earlier in May, and on the 18th they had advanced quickly up the Bakri Ridge by night to Hajib. They had halted there for a few days; then they had advanced again, attacking and driving back a party of dissidents as they went.

While they were preparing for their final advance we were preparing for an advance up the Wadi Misra. Our operation proved abortive. We were to advance right up the wadi for six miles, and then on to the Jebel Huriyah beyond. We were to clear the wadi as we went so that guns and supply convoys could move up it. Providing a road-head for supplies at the end of the Misra would reduce the pressure on the helicopters; and a gun position there could cover most of the remaining mountains.

With X Company gone we had only two companies; but we were to operate in conjunction with 2nd Bn FRA, and we had a mixed squadron of tanks and armoured cars under command.

It was an impressive valley, long and more or less straight, with a line of hills rising 1,500 feet or more very steeply on each side. The FRA were to take the right hills, Y Company the left, and Z Company, now commanded by Major 'Jungle' Baizley, the wadi itself. We would climb both shoulders of the valley by night and move along both crests by night. Z Company would push along the wadi bottom, getting into villages before first light, with the armour following by day to support and re-supply them.

According to their CO, the FRA had been immensely impressed at seeing the Commando move off into the darkness on our first night advance and at hearing of our successful climbs. They were determined to show that they could do this kind of thing at least as well. This they did, but not with us. Our operation never happened.

In the late afternoon of the 25th, as we were forming up, the first great rains fell in the hills some miles to the north, and a flood swept down the Wadi Rabwa, lying across our path. Within minutes the dry wadi was filled to eight feet or more with a torrent. We were lucky, as most of the unit were on high ground; only some of our echelon vehicles, not connected with the night's operation, were turned over. One vehicle near Y Company was caught in the flood, and only quick and gallant work by Ted Goddard and the CSM, MacVicar, saved the two men in it. Goddard got to it with a rope and brought them off; within seconds the Landrover turned over and was swept downstream.

As the floods began to subside, almost as quickly as they had risen, I sent a patrol across the river. hey returned, wet to the eyebrows, but said that the river was crossable and that the water was still falling. As H Hour approached we formed up and waited for a report from the FRA, who had been out of radio contact since the floods began.

The report came in, saying that FRA had been hit badly by the floods. In remarkable short time they had sorted themselves out and were loping cheerfully towards their start line. However the Brigadier postponed the operation for twenty-four hours – as

One of the Landrovers firmly stuck in the mud after the floods

Ted Goddard (rear) surveys one of the Landrovers which was washed away down the wadi and overturned. Scout cars and 3-tonners were also affected

he put it, with trouble even before we had crossed the start line there were the makings of a fine mess up.

On the 26th it was postponed again, because of a battle developing in the Wadi Dhubsan. That evening we sat outside our mess-tent at Thumier as the sun went down, drinking moodily and staring at the hills we were supposed to be climbing. Next afternoon the Brigadier told me that the operation was cancelled, as we and 3rd Parachute Battalion were to be withdrawn from the Radfan. All the men of the unit were keyed up for the operation, and this was dismal news, so I got permission to patrol in strength into the Wadi Misra. That night I took out the whole unit. We got on to the high hills on each side, and Z Company penetrated 3,000 yards up the wadi. We were out again by first light. It served no purpose except to let off steam and to provide some realistic training, but it seemed necessary at the time. On 28 May I sent the unit back to Little Aden, and waited at Thumier for X Company to return from their action in the Wadi Dhubsan.

3rd Parachute Battalion had reached Arnold's Spur, the southern tip of the Bakri Ridge, and on 25 May they were poised there for a dramatic raid into the Wadi Dhubsan. Mike Banks and X Company joined them, flown up by helicopter. There were logistic difficulties, high winds or heavy rain or swirling mist limiting the time that helicopters could operate, or cutting short a flying programme at a critical moment. The difficulties were overcome by hard and dangerous flying and by the usual furious energy of the paratroopers, and on the evening on the 25th final plans were laid.

Our old friends 815 Squadron from HMS *Centaur* had arrived at Thumier for a short stay to give the Belvederes a well-earned rest in Aden. They were allotted to support the operation. The Wessex were smaller and nippier than the Belvederes, and though their payload in the high mountains was small they worked very hard and displayed their usual dash.

The Wadi Dhubsan was a strange slice of country. Looking from the top of Arnold's Spur the ground dropped steeply for 1,700 feet into the wadi bottom. To the left, a mile away across a narrow and jagged ridge was a pointed hill called Jebel Sababa. To the right and also a mile away was a strange flat feature a mile long and with steep sides, a mesa, called Jebel Haqla. The wadi itself was narrow and had steep sides and several subsidiary wadis and ridges jutting into it. There was a prominent ridge on the north side leading down from Jebel Sababa, and another opposite it about 1,000 yards east of Jebel Haqla.

The full story of this dramatic raid belongs to 3rd Bn Parachute Regiment, and I will describe only X Company's part, in the event an important one.

The raid began on the night 25/26 May. One company of 3rd Para moved over to the Jebel Haqla and the other made the appalling climb down into the Wadi Dhubsan. There was a kind of bowl at the west end of the Dhubsan, and they secured this, putting picquets on low subsidiary ridges facing down the Dhubsan. At 0800 hours X Company were concentrated at the eastern end of the bowl, and soon afterwards advanced beyond the line of picquets, along the bottom of the silent and apparently empty valley, with orders to comb the wadi as far as a bend 1,000 yards ahead.

At 0725 hours there had been a report of fifty dissidents approaching the Dhubsan from the south. Up to the time the advance began there had been no shooting, but Mike Banks picquetted the low intermediate ridges as best he could. It was slow and hot work.

When they had covered about 600 yards the leading section saw a group of five dissidents high above them on the right of the valley. They opened fire and saw two of them fall, to be helped behind a large rock by the others. Very soon afterwards firing broke out from high up on the right, followed by more firing from the left. X Company took cover and returned the fire, but had difficulty in locating exactly where the fire was coming from. They began moving forward from cover to cover and trying to gain higher ground. The fire-fight became heavier as more dissidents joined in. Control of the company was getting ever more difficult with sections deployed as picquets on the low ridges and other sections working their way along the hillsides.

A Scout helicopter flew over X Company and into the fire of the dissidents, was hit, and force-landed just behind the leading men of X Company. The leading troops dashed further forward to get well beyond it, while the pilot and passengers got out and under cover, and the shooting got heavier still. By this time the whole company was under fire from enemy in concealed positions high above them, to the front and on both sides, which they could only reach by a long uphill climb. Air strikes were called in to attack the dissident's positions with rockets and cannon. The second-in-command, Captain Roger Brind, ran out into a patch of open ground to lay fluorescent panels to control the air strikes, and was shot through the stomach. He was quickly brought back under cover, but he had laid the panels.

Up on the right, James Barr and part of 1 Troop was under heavy fire from the front and right, and for a short time from the rear as well. A Marine was badly wounded, and another, shot through the chest, died almost immediately as he was being pulled under cover by James Barr. Corporal Watson was within striking distance of two buildings overlooking the final wadi bend, and he moved his section across the broken hillside under cover of smoke and got into the buildings.

X Company's naval medical orderly, SBA Wade, was moving about the wadi bottom escorted by a young Marine, disregarding the enemy fire as he gave first aid to the wounded.

So it went on. Much of the time X Company could not see the dissidents above them at all, and located them as best they could by the sound of firing. Occasionally a sangar would be located and heavy fire brought on to it, and sometimes air strikes, artillery and mortars on top of Arnold's Spur would join in, but the firing continued as X Company worked their way slowly forward.

For most of the morning X Company had been fighting on their own, but during the course of the day the paratroopers had been working along the higher ground, and as they moved in closer and above the dissidents the firing died away. X Company reorganised and got their wounded out.

That night the paratroopers patrolled forward beyond the wadi bend and met no one. The Scout was repaired, by miraculous work with a blowtorch under a screen, and it flew out next morning. The battalion began the long climb back on to the Bakri Ridge.

I was at Thumier airfield when the wounded were brought out by helicopter. X Company had lost one killed and three very badly wounded. 3rd Parachute Battalion had lost five wounded, including the RSM, badly wounded but boundlessly cheerful. The wounded were whisked back by air to the RAF hospital in Aden; they were there within a couple of hours of being picked up by helicopter in the Dhubsan. It was a long cry from the campaign of 1903, when the soldier wounded in the Radfan had had to survive a camel journey to Aden.

On 28 May I met Mike Banks and X Company when they were flown into Thumier by helicopter. They were very cheerful. When they were asked about 'the rough time' they had had, their main recollection was of the heavy rain on Bakri Ridge. Memories were short. Next day X Company moved up to Dhala, where there was more shooting.

Chapter 11

In the High Mountains

June passed with little to distinguish it from any other month except that we gave ourselves more leave. Every man was entitled to fourteen days leave a year, but we had given little leave since November because of the pressure of events and training. We now gave as much leave as we could to the 'old hands' while the rest trained. With a final exhortation to the rest of the unit to train hard, I went on leave.

We were Middle East Reserve Battalion again. We heard, a little enviously, of the work the other units were doing in the Radfan, and we never doubted that sooner or later we would return to the mountains. We guessed that it might be sooner. We talked to those who came down from the Radfan after us; and when the SAS came down at the end of their splendid tour there, we brought them into our camp and looked after them before they returned to England.

Among the other work and preparations necessary for the Reserve Battalion, we continued to train for the Radfan. There was one thing I particularly wanted to test. We had learnt to get on to the hilltops at night, and had developed techniques for dealing with any trouble we might meet on the way; but, having reached the hilltops by first light, we must be able to exploit quickly to catch any dissidents below us – hard and hot work searching the rough hillsides.

This problem was tied up with a state known as 'heat exhaustion'. Through loss of salt and liquid in the great heat, the body temperature rises suddenly and cannot be relieved by sweating. We had suffered little from this. Until we went into the Radfan there had been only one recorded case in the unit, a newly arrived and over-weight sergeant on a hard march along the coast: we had been successfully treated by being thrown into the sea. There had been few, if any, real cases during our operations in the Radfan, and I suspected that there was a large moral factor in it. The condition undoubtedly existed the more people got it. It was akin to the 'battle neurosis' of war: there were men who would crack under the strain of battle, and more would no doubt crack under great and continuous strain. But whenever battle neurosis was accepted as an honourable way out of battle, a trickle of men on the borderline would develop appropriate symptoms. If you made it clear that most men were often tired and not a little frightened, and that battle neurosis – whatever its cause in an honest case – was a sign of weakness, the trickle stopped.

Similarly with heat exhaustion. Frequently the whole unit would be hot, tired and thirsty. Some would be literally exhausted, as one might be on a hard exercise in

England. If heat exhaustion was too easily accepted, men near the end of their tether would clutch at the phrase and collapse. Most of the unit might one day be near the end of its tether, and we could not afford to carry men who could still walk.

The exercise was not designed to test heat exhaustion, or even to risk it, but to see how fast and how hard we could move at first light after a hard night's climb. It was held in the hills behind Little Aden; lower than the Radfan but a tough climb on the routes I chose and a difficult advance along knife-edge ridges. The exercise only lasted twelve hours, but the valley was hotter than the Radfan, the air still and humid: a three mile night march over soft sand and a stiff climb; a night advance along the crest, and then operating along the crests and steep hillsides well into the heat of the day, fully laden and working on three water bottles each.

We had twenty casualties: some of them the inevitable minor sprains and twists from falls in the dark; most were from the heat. All were got back to camp quickly and none had serious after effects. The number diagnosed as heat exhaustion was five. The rest were without question exhausted. The rest of the unit was still going strong in the hottest part of the day.

A check afterwards produced the inevitable crop of men who had not rested before the exercise, and a few who had drunk too much beer the day before. However it was a harsh and timely reminder that the borders of heat exhaustion were not far away.

Plenty of water and salt was the standard method of preventing heat exhaustion. In the mountains you could not be sure of plenty of water, and salt on its own was not much use. We always carried salt tablets with us, but one company commander said that hot tea at the right time was worth a trainload of salt tablets. Justifiable exaggeration. Heat exhaustion was a real problem, a physiological state; but there was a broad borderline where the problem lay in the mind.

On 2 July we returned to the Radfan. For the outside world the high drama had ended with the capture of Cap Badge and the raid into the Wadi Dhubsan. For the units who had remained, and now for us, there was plenty of hard work and not a little drama.

Our place in the Wadi Misra had been taken by the Royal Anglians, and they and 22nd FRA had advanced along the crests and wadi bottom. On 7 June the dissidents had foolishly stayed to fight at the head of the Wadi Misra, and had suffered heavy casualties from air strikes and gunfire before withdrawing under pressure from the two units. This was the final and decisive battle of the Radfan campaign. Soon afterwards the Royal Anglians and the FRA advanced again, and on 11 June, after a night march, the flags of 2nd Bn FRA and the Royal Anglians were hoisted side by side on the top of the Jebel Huriyah, the highest peak in the Radfan.

The valley of the Wadi Taim had been worked over by the FRA and the King's Own Scottish Borderers. In late June they had picquetted the hills astride 'Pilgrim's Way', a wadi leading southwards into the mountains. At the end of the month a company of FRA made the astonishing night climb on to the Jebel Widina, 2,300 feet from the wadi bottom. They found the hill deserted.

When we arrived in early July we found a very different kind of war from the one we had begun in early May. The main dissident resistance had been broken by the capture of the high hills in the Wadi Taim and in the south, and all the tribes had gone. They were to remain out until they accepted the terms of the Federal Government, and our job was to keep them out.

The dissidents had fallen back on typical guerrilla operations. They moved through the hills by day or night, parties of a dozen men, to snipe at the positions or to lay mines on the newly built tracks along which the supply vehicles moved. At times they even sniped at the picquets around the Thumier base itself. They had lost the first phase, the pretence of a great new 'liberation front' in the Radfan, and lost much face in the process. They hoped to recover their prestige by inflicting casualties on the FRA and the British. They also hoped, no doubt, that their steady pressure would force the deployment of large numbers of troops in a long an expensive campaign; and this campaign, in conjunction with the 'fronts' that they were hoping to open elsewhere, would over-extend and tire out the British and Arab troops.

It is a difficult form of warfare to counter, for the guerrillas hold the initiative, and in this case they had a wide area of choice – my unit had an area of forty square miles, most of it difficult mountains and narrow valleys. They can strike when and where they choose; even if they withdraw for a week to rest, the troops may not know it and must remain alert and active as if the guerrillas were still operating.

The best way to recover the initiative is to attack the guerrilla base or to deprive them of supplies. Here the guerrilla base was in more mountains, outside the area in which we could operate; and their supplies forwarded from their base were carried on their backs or hidden in the many hundreds of small caves and underground stores hidden throughout the Radfan.

There are many other ways of dealing with guerrillas, and many were tried in the Radfan. One effective way is to kill dissidents – to make the occupational risk of being a guerrilla so great that many retire from the game, the rest becoming over-cautious and even timid.

They could either be hunted or they could be ambushed. I had little faith in patrols moving by day in this kind of country: the sharp-eyed hill-men would spot the patrols first, and disappear. The best chance was to ambush – small parties spread through the mountains, lying up for perhaps two or three days at a time, waiting for a fleeting shot at a dissident, by day or by night. If we could get a few 'kills' and reduce their power, it might even add to the internal dissensions that are so common among undisciplined guerrillas.

We did many different things during this and our next tour in the Radfan. Most of the rest of this book deals with our main task – the attempts to capture or kill dissidents by ambush.

First, though, we had another job. Just as the dissidents wished to force us to deploy as many troops as possible, we wished to deploy as few as possible, so that the battalions could be rested in turn and no other troops need be called in. The Force HQ and the administrative troops would not get much of a break from the Radfan: they at least had some comforts around them in Thumier. The battalions must be rested in turn. We could not afford to hold every hilltop. To keep the dissidents guessing the Brigadier, now Brigadier Chandos Blair, OBE, MC – Brigadier Blacker had returned to England on promotion – decided to move the units around the hills. He also decided to search the Wadi Dhubsan, not visited since 3rd Parachute Battalion's raid a month before.

The troops had left the Bakri Ridge and Arnold's Spur some time ago, and I was told to search the wadi starting from the opposite end. We would have to approach from the Jebel Huriyah and the Jebel Widina, picquet the sides of the valley and move westwards towards Arnold's Spur. There was nothing to show that the valley was occupied, but a few men could cause a lot of trouble. It would have to be done properly.

X Company was still busy at Dhala so I only had two companies. I took one look at the Dhubsan; decided I needed three companies, and told John Lloyd that he had to turn Support Company into a rifle company at twenty-four hours notice. Poor John! I did this to him often – rifle company in Tanganyika, riot platoon in Aden, now a rifle company again; yet I always expected him to produce his mortars and machine guns and mobats and fire them as if he never did anything else. He muttered into his moustache and went away to think it over. I managed to extricate 1 Troop (James Barr again) from X Company to help him out. In the event we had no trouble in the Dhubsan, but it is worth recording as the toughest march the unit did in the Radfan and perhaps typical of the problems of mountain warfare.

On 3 July Y and Support Companies drove to the entrance to Pilgrim's Way, where they bivouacked for the night, soaked by a heavy rainstorm. Soon after the first light they marched three miles up the wadi, climbed 2,300 feet up Jebel Widina, and rested.

We had had no time to reconnoitre routes, so during the night the Reconnaissance Troop (now commanded by Ted Goddard, formerly second-in-command of Y Company) went over to the Jebel Sababa to reconnoitre the route down the long spur leading into the Dhubsan – the same one from which X Company had been fired upon during their previous visit. It was a black night; they tried for five hours, reaching down with their rifles to find footholds below them, but made little progress – going downhill, by night or day, was often as difficult as going up.

Jebel Widina, Jebel Sababah and Arnold's Spur viewed from 'Cap Badge'

They tried again when the moon came up in the early morning, found a route, and moved down the spur followed by Support and Y Companies. Support dropped off picquets as they went, and by late afternoon the north side of the Dhubsan was picquetted and Y Company was on a ridge near the bottom ready for the next day's search.

To the south, Z Company had had an even tougher march. On 3 July they bivouacked at the south end of the Wadi Misra. On the 4th they climbed Jebel Huriyah and moved over to their start line on a cliff facing the Jebel Haqla two miles away. That night they went across a ridge to the Jebel Haqla – tolerably easy by day but difficult by night. 'Movement Light' was provided by powerful flares dropped from Shackletons, their position controlled from Commando HQ. Even so there were long periods of blackness, and black shadows even when the flares were up.

One man disappeared over a cliff, and there was an agonising pause until a flow of reprehensible but understandable language floated quietly up to the anxious listeners. By first light the company was on Jebel Haqla, and two troops were moving down the long slope to the east, where they found picquet positions covering the south side of the Dhubsan. By this time some of the men had been moving almost continuously for thirty hours.

The search was uneventful. Both Z and Support Companies found positions from which the dissidents had fired at X Company in the wadi bottom, well concealed sangars with empty cartridge cases and discarded kit. Y Company spent two hot days searching the villages and hillsides in the Dhubsan, moving towards Arnold's Spur, with new picquets put out above to cover them as they advanced. They got close to the foot of Arnold's Spur, but not a shot was fired. Later on the 7th Y Company were flown out by Peter Hart and his Belvederes, and the rest marched back to the top of their mountains – Support Company to Jebel Widina, Y and Z on Jebel Haqla.

Not all the rest: I had been told to establish bases on the Jebels Widina and Haqla from which I was to patrol into the surrounding country. Patrolling from the hilltops into the wadi bottoms would be an exhausting business. I decided to leave the Reconnaissance Troop lying up in the bottom of the Dhubsan for a week. This produced our first successful ambush.

The Reconnaissance Troop had been organised into a HQ and two sections of eight men each. It was trained and equipped to move greater distances independently and to 'lie up' for longer than the rifle troops.

While the search of the Dhubsan was going on I told Ted Goddard (the Troop Commander) to find himself a nice village. He found his village on a slight rise on the south side of the Dhubsan due south of Jebel Widina and stocked it up with food and water. On 7 July the Recce Troop disappeared discreetly into the village. The rest of the troops withdrew to their hilltops, leaving the Recce Troop alone, with the nearest support four hours march away.

There were a dozen houses, small and ramshackle, low ceilings and small windows, the tiny rooms stuffy and dirty and bug-ridden. The staircases, for what they were worth, were on the outside of the buildings. The Recce Troop stayed in their rooms all day, sweating, preparing observation holes, sleeping as best they could. Each night they crept out to meet for conferences and to prepare the administration for the next day; and each night they sent patrols into the surrounding wadis.

One such patrol was 'call sign eight zero bravo' (8OB), eight men led by Sergeant Munson, a tough individualist, formerly of the Special Boats Section. On 11 July he led his patrol down to the junction of the Wadis Dhubsan and Dura'a, then a mile up the Wadi Dura'a to a small group of houses chosen from an air photograph, looking down into the wadi. They were to lie up there all day and return next night.

In the morning two armed dissidents appeared, moving cautiously along the wadi. They were not a good target and were too far away to intercept, so Sergeant Munson held his fire. They disappeared. Munson was about to move out again to stalk them when they appeared again, about 400 yards away. He gave the order and both men were shot down in the first volley. One of them was killed outright; the other disappeared behind cover and returned the fire. Some scattered shots also came from across the wadi, but the dissident was located and shot.

All was quiet. Whoever else had fired was either waiting or had gone. We wanted to get the bodies back for identification. Y Company, on the Jebel Haqla, had a patrol base on a hill 1,000 yards north of Munson. A Scout helicopter was sent to us, and we quickly reinforced that base by ferrying men down from Haqla. Meanwhile a patrol from the base moved out to a hill above Munson's section. Under their protection Munson took a party down to the wadi – such was the country that it took them an hour to cover the 400 yards – and carried the bodies to cover. The Scout dipped quickly into the wadi, the bodies were put into the back, the mail delivered for the troop, and the Scout returned to Thumier.

The bodies were identified: one was wanted particularly for the murder of a Federal Guard soldier in Thumier some time before; the other was known to have fought in one of the battles of the Wadi Rabwa. This was one of the few times in the whole Radfan campaign that the bodies of dead dissidents were recovered.

The ambush was perhaps typical of the kind of work we had before us. Patrols would lie up for day after day, not a man having a sight of a dissident. Then a chance would come, usually fleeting and at long range. If the patrol, usually tired and very bored, did not take the chance, it was gone. I had given orders that the dissidents were to be captured if possible. We never got within catching distance.

Two nights later the Recce Troop climbed out of the Dhubsan and up on to the Jebel Widina. Our natural delight at seeing them well and cheerful was marred by one thing. They stank.

Just before this, on 13 July, we had got another 'kill', though we did not know it for sure at the time.

After Z Company had climbed back on to the Jebel Haqla, I had told Baizley that he was to take Z Company over to Arnold's Spur to establish a patrol base there. Lieutenant Ian Martin – he who had led at Tanganyika – spent two nights reconnoitring routes. On the night 10/11 July Z Company moved across, again led by Ian Martin. It was a relatively easy march, as marches went in that country, but they could not find the way leading up over the cliff face on Arnold's Spur. Ian found the way up with a small reconnaissance party, and the rest of the company was brought up over a rope. Z Company based themselves on Arnold's Spur and began searching the Bakri Ridge.

Just before dark on 12 July, Y Company, on the Jebel Haqla, spotted twelve men in a wadi to their west heading northwards towards the Bakri Ridge. The men were in the area of a friendly tribe, but they were watched. As dusk fell they were seen heading out of the friendly area. Z Company put ambushes along the Bakri Ridge, but no contact was made that night.

Next day Baizley, acting on a hunch, took a strong patrol along the ridge to Hajib and searched the village, and then began to search the Hajib Feature, a shelf sticking out from the east side of the Bakri Ridge and tilting upwards, an area of broad, open terracing.

After some hours searching, an observation post in Hajib reported seeing four armed men in a village on the feature. Ian Martin stalked the village with his troop and got within 100 yards, intent on capturing the dissidents if he could. He was just getting his cut-off parties into position when the dissidents took alarm and ran. The troop rushed the village and saw the dissidents disappearing over the side of the feature. They fired, but as they did so more firing broke out to their north. Another, larger, group of dissidents was in the same buildings high up on the tilted plateau. Part of the other troop was caught in the open, and one Marine was slightly wounded in the hand. Martin counter-attacked, and one dissident, seen fleetingly, was hit by automatic fire and seen to fall.

The dissidents had a commanding position in their fort-like houses, built to dominate those terraces. The firefight increased as the troops tried to work in closer. Artillery was brought into action, and gunfire came down accurately on the houses where the dissidents were, but the dissident firing continued.

The only approach was up the steep slope towards the houses, likely to be expensive and pointless: as ever, the dissidents would slip away over the side of the hill. I called Z Company off, to rest and 'water-up'.

After dark they sent in a fighting patrol which rocketed and searched the houses – an empty gesture, as we had little doubt that they would be gone. At least we now held the upper rim of the plateau and could search at our leisure.

There followed a three-day hunt. At first light Z Company found two lots of bloodstains and a trail of blood leading to the north and ending in some scrub. Next day there was a report from one of our observation posts of two men seen near a house in the bottom of a nearby wadi. After last light a patrol surrounded and searched the house – no dissidents but more bloodstains. Another reported sighting and another abortive search; ambushes lay up at night on all the likely escape routes.

At the end of three days I called Z Company off. A few days later a report came in through the market place in Thumier one dissident dead and another badly wounded.

An unpleasant kind of manhunt, with the odds on our side. There were risks, though. Searching a house at night is at best difficult; and in an Arab house, with its tiny, dark rooms, small doors and narrow winding stairs, a most hazardous business. Once, a patrol heard noises in a room, resisted the temptation to throw a grenade, flashed a torch. Inside were three old women, left behind when the tribes had gone. Stocks of grain were found in the house. The old women were left there, with some of the Marines' spare rations.

At that time I rescinded my previous order, and said that troops could move in the bottom of the valley by daylight without picquets above them, provided there was cover not too far away and they had water to last until dusk. Even with small patrols of six men it was a reasonable risk, and the changed circumstances and with our greater experience of this kind of work. The dissidents were reported to be moving in parties of a dozen, so the patrols had to be careful. And a risk it was, as we found out later.

Z Company continued their patrolling and moved up and down the Bakri Ridge like a yo-yo, following up the flimsiest report from the friendly Arabs nearby or the slightest trace on the ground, with ambushes out every night and patrols following up by day. They ambushed one cow.

We brought in Scout helicopters to help the rapid deployment of the company to cover a sighting, and worked out a drill: the company commander would leap in with a sergeant with a radio and GPMG group (light machine gun), case the area, drop off the sergeant's party, then return to fly in his reserves by Scout. Our 'tame' Scout pilot at that time was Captain Bob Holmeshaw, he who had picked up the dead dissidents from the Wadi Dura'a.

Z Company turned their attention to the complex of wadis between the Bakri Ridge and the Jebel Widina, particularly to Pilgrim's Way, long since deserted by the picquets that had covered us on our march to the Jebel Widina. It was hard patrolling country, and ambushes were often out for three nights, sometimes four, carrying everything they needed. They sometimes collected water from the occasional pools in the wadi bottoms, or from wells; but this meant part of the night lost reaching the spot and protecting it while water was drawn. It was better to carry five water bottles; once in the ambush position the men could avoid sweating too much by lying still, or as still as they could under the attention of the insects. The night moves to the ambush position was the most difficult part, and even with their great experience of the night many men came back with shirts or trousers ripped apart. Boots lasted only a few weeks in this country.

The only chance came, fleetingly, and this was missed. There were two small ambush parties in Pilgrim's Way, 1,000 yards apart. Two men were covering one of the water holes in the wadi. One morning a group of dissidents suddenly appeared about 200 yards from the water hole, spotted the two men, and fled. The men opened fire and the rest of the ambush moved out across the open ground to intercept, but it was too late: they had disappeared, as they always did. This was typical: seven days of ambushing and waiting, and the chance came for a few seconds. During those few seconds one of the men must have been careless and moved, and the chance was gone.

Back on Bakri Ridge the drill worked out with the Scout was put into action. The Scout arrived, Baizley and his team leapt in, and they flew high over the area. We had discussed the escape routes from this ambush position, and Baizley chose one, made a wide detour, and came in to land on the blind side of a ridge overlooking the wadi. As the Scout went into the hover it was hit in the fuel tank by an explosive bullet and the helicopter filled with fumes. Bob Holmeshaw did some fast thinking and some fast juggling and slid the helicopter just over the brow and into the valley beyond, as the power began to fail. They swept right over the ambush position, with fuel streaming out behind – pained report of 'helicopter flying dangerously low over our position'.

The helicopter skimmed down Pilgrim's Way into the Wadi Taim and landed at an airstrip, Baizley and his team did the fastest exit ever recorded, and then strolled back sheepishly to where Bob was methodically doing the switching off drill. His only comment: 'Well, we've joined the Club'.

The search went on for the rest of the day, the picquets on the mountain tops made one or two brief sightings, but it looked as though the dissidents had got away. However it was perhaps those same dissidents that ran into a Support Company ambush next day.

After they had picquetted the Dhubsan, Support Company had returned to the top of the Jebel Widina. Commando HQ was there too, and there we remained as long as we could; for all the hills we saw in the Radfan the Jebel Widina was the most comfortable, the most attractive and the most peaceful. It was two miles long and almost flat on top – so flat that we flew a Landrover up there by Belvedere and used it for ferrying stores about the plateau. The sides were almost sheer in most places; there were few approaches to guard and not much chance of interruption by dissidents. The air was tolerably cool by day – for those who were not climbing – and by night the place was cool enough to merit a blanket. In the late afternoon there were often high winds and heavy rainstorms, and sometimes the worst thunderstorms I have ever known, though these were usually over quickly.

The view was marvellous. All around was as startling and dramatic a landscape as one could wish to see – great bare mountains, jagged slopes, isolated houses and small villages on pinnacles high above the wadis, with, in places, narrow cultivated terraces nicked out of the rocky hill-sides extending from the wadi bottom up to the houses. Far below us were the wadis, sometimes with narrow stretches of green cultivation beside them. They looked very beautiful. And they looked a long way to walk.

The flat top of the Jebel Widina provided a useful base for operations. Every few days an Argosy or Beverley would fly over and drop our main supplies by parachute, to save the overworked Belvederes. We would collect the supplies and parachutes to a central dump, and from this dump the supplies would be run out by Landrover to the picquets round the Widina, or by Scout to the picquets on the more difficult hills – sometimes to tiny Landing Sites only a few feet wide and with hazards from the erratic air currents among the hills.

I liked Jebel Widina. John Lloyd and Support Company did not like it at all, as they had to get off it and get down among the remote wadis.

When they first got back on the Widina they were still organised as a rifle company. As part of their territory was out of artillery range I told John that he would need his mortars and machine guns again. He said they were already packed up at Thumier ready to be flown forward. I thanked him for his foresight and sent some direct to Z Company, with the men to man them. John looked glum again, but contrived to put picquets in key places around the Widina and still had enough men for patrolling – the picquets did double duty, with their mortars or Vickers beside them; and John got his revenge on me by insisting that Commando HQ, at the south-west corner of the Widina, should constitute one of the picquets.

'The view was marvellous'

The landscape around the Widina was magnificent but difficult, in some ways the most difficult we saw in the Radfan. Leading away from the plateau were saw-edge ridges with deep sides. Moving along the sides of the ridges was dangerous and slow; moving along the top, the saw-edge, often worse, with sheer drops or steep climbs. It was not impossible to move. The problem was not merely finding ways down into the wadis, but finding ways that were good enough to allow an ambush to move silently by night without too much expenditure of energy and water.

After several days and several climbing accidents, most fortunately minor, ways were found. James Barr's troop, still attached to Support Company, searched a wadi to the east, drawing a blank.

They went down there again, by night, the day before the unsuccessful ambush in Pilgrim's Way, and pushed out over a mile from the Widina to lie up in a village. There was a pass leading into the wadi from the north, and we thought this might be a route for the dissidents. After the failure in Pilgrim's Way the ambush was ordered to cover that approach.

On the morning after the ambush in Pilgrim's Way two dissidents appeared from this pass, and were shot down at 350 yards in the first volley. Two more appeared almost immediately, and one was hit and wounded, possibly the other too.

I gave orders that the patrol was to go out to find the wounded men. Barr left a section in the buildings and took the rest of the patrol across the wadi and past the two bodies. They searched for a while and found nothing. Shooting then began from further east, and the troop returned fire. The firing became heavier, from long range but coming unpleasantly close, and Barr's troop took cover.

The mortars went into action, but the dissidents were just out of range. A Vickers gun was flown by Scout to the tip of the lower plateau of Jebel Widina, to the east, and this brought down accurate fire. As ever, the problem was locating the enemy. It sometimes took half-an-hour before a sniper was spotted.

Recce troop were flown down to the lower plateau – it was too risky to permit Scouts to be flown to the wadi bottom – and they moved quickly down the slopes and along the wadi to join Barr's troop, and then got on to what high ground they could.

Then the proceedings took an ominous turn. Because of the lie of the ground, the dissidents could get on to the high ground above the ambush, and we could not get along the knife-edge above them. The danger was not great, as both troops were well concealed, but there was not much future in it. I called the ambush off. After dark they make the long climb back on to Jebel Widina, bring with them a bandolier with some explosive bullets in it.

That was the last we saw of the dissidents during that stay in the Radfan. Five weeks: only four definite contacts: five dissidents killed and two or three wounded.

It had been a long and hard time for everyone. Most men of the rifle companies had lain in ambush at least half their nights. Many had not seen a dissident the whole time, had done nothing but wait and watch – and climb over the hills at night and get thirsty and dirty. Somehow most enjoyed it, the work of the small team infinitely more satisfying than the impersonal momentum of a whole unit on the move. There were young corporals who would spot a likely dissident route during a day patrol and would ask – and usually get – permission to ambush it the next night.

There were feats of endurance too. To me the most impressive was a quiet one: a young corporal who took a section out on his own before dawn on one of the searches, moved all day tracking and searching, and returned long after dark – having drunk less than one water bottle per man.

Our respect for the dissidents remained high. They were not afraid of our superior numbers and firepower. They could move over the hills far faster than we could, and when things got difficult they would just disappear. Much of it, of course, was the traditional and very real advantage of dissidents fighting on their own ground: and they could decide what, if anything, they were going to do, and when they were going to do it. Here, in the high mountains, their own ground, they had achieved nothing against us, because we were usually above them, a position they respected; or we moved by night, something we were far better at than they were.

We became convinced of our superiority over the dissidents at this kind of work. This may seem a strange claim, when we had artillery and mortars and air strikes to support us. It was not that kind of war at all. At the point of contact there were parties of six or eight Marines, on their own for three days and nights, perhaps six hours march from the nearest help, moving over strange ground into dark and silent villages: against them were parties of dissidents, armed as well as the Marines, moving over ground they knew well. It was nice to have the mortars and machine guns there, to exploit a success or to support a failure. But at the point and moment of contact it was a straight fight.

Yet, on the two occasions when the dissidents were fighting from their traditional positions – the commanding buildings on the Hajib Feature and the ground above the wadi east of Jebel Widina – I was content to let them be. There was no key ground to be won, only an exchange of casualties for little purpose; and time was on our side.

Time was already running out for the dissidents, in this phase at least. Before we left the Radfan the tribes were making their first overtures for peace and a return to their villages. The dissidents had made them great promises, which they had not fulfilled. The FRA and the British were sitting on the mountains and around the fertile plains, and we showed signs of staying there as long as we wished.

Chapter 12

The Valley of the Taim

We were tired when we got back to camp, but we knew enough about Aden not to expect too much rest; which was lucky, as we didn't get any at all. There had been terrorist attacks in Aden, and the units not committed in the Radfan had new duties to bear. Within 48 hours a troop was on guard at Government House, another was on anti-terrorist patrols, a third on 'stand-by' close to Aden – a whole company swallowed up each night. With only two rifle companies – X were busy at Dhala – it meant that the rifle troops were out of their beds every other night, as they had been in the Radfan.

On patrol in the Wadi Taim

I needed more men. I looked at John Lloyd, and he sighed and put away his mortars and machine guns and practised riot drill. Even so this was only enough to plug the gaps. Happily we were only in Little Aden for seventeen days, and on 23 August we went back to the Radfan, this time to occupy the Danaba Basin and the valley of the Wadi Taim.

The valley is ten miles long and up to four miles wide. At the western end is the Rabwa Pass. At the eastern end the wadi passes through low hills and a narrow gorge into the Wadi Bana, a wide wadi and a trade route leading south to the plains. The north side is bounded by the high hills of the Halmain, a tribe now established as friendly; to the south, equally abruptly by the foothills leading up to the Bakri Ridge and the mountains we had recently left.

The dissidents had been busy in the valley, and peering down from our mountain tops we had seen almost every night the streaks of tracer and flashes of gunfire. Except for Cap Badge and the hills around it the valley looked deceptively flat, and we had decided that ambushing dissidents there would be easy.

The previous unit had been ambushing and patrolling heavily along the tracks, and there had not been a single incident of mining during their whole tour in the valley. On the other hand their patrols had had only one fleeting contact with dissidents, at long range and indecisive. They had tried many things and many devices for catching the dissidents. As the CO put it, they 'had run out of ideas'.

I had used exactly the same expression a fortnight before leaving the mountains. A CO deployed his companies, gave them areas for patrolling, visited the companies to discuss progress, and occasionally ordered a special task or adjusted boundaries. Patrolling of this kind seldom brings immediate dividends. You have to decide on a pattern, a network of patrols and ambushes in the area. If that pattern is sound you may, in the course of time, and if you are lucky, get a number of contacts. As a CO there is little you can do once the pattern is made and running well, except be patient. You must let it run for a reasonable time. There is a limit to the number of refinements you can make. As a CO you run out of ideas. It is up to the company commanders, until such time as your intuition tells you that the pattern is wrong, or the circumstances have changed.

At that time I was full of ideas, and so were the company commanders. In this flat ground, without the awful hills to cross, we were going to kill a lot of dissidents, and quickly.

We learnt that it was not so easy.

The valley was guarded from four patrol bases: Monk's Field, in the Danaba Basin; Paddy's Field two miles east of Cap Badge; 'Table Top' – which looked like its name: 300 foot high, a mile long and quite flat – guarding the south side; and Blair's Field further east where the valley began to narrow. They were small, tented camps on slightly raised ground, with stone walls round the tents or round the camps. Close by each camp airstrips levelled by the Sappers could take Twin Pioneers. Life here was comfortable. Aircraft brought in fresh rations each day; local water supplies had been found, and showers had been rigged; there were tents for most men, camp beds, sleeping bags; and mail came in regularly. War in the Radfan was getting soft.

The Twin Pioneers that came into the landing strips each morning could not bring enough for all our needs; and anyway there was always the risk that the aircraft would be called away for other urgent business.

The Sappers had built a net of roads from Thumier leading through the Rabwa Pass to all the bases in the Wadi Taim, and we used these roads for heavy re-supply convoys and for minor routine trips. It was against these roads that the dissidents directed their most successful form of activity – mining.

The road, built by the Sappers, leading to the Wadi Taim

Mining had long been a feature of life among the mountains. It was easy for the dissidents to hide in the hills close to the narrow roads, often in the wadi bottoms, and slip out at night to lay their mines. They laid them well – well concealed and well sited; and deep, so that they could not be located by mine detectors, and often did not explode until several vehicles had passed over them and compacted the ground.

There were no certain measures that we could take against the mines. Ferret Scout Cars would usually lead convoys, in the hope that the mines would go up under these armoured vehicles. In September the dissidents began to use the British Mark 7 mine, more powerful and able to blow a Ferret clean off the road. The bottom of every vehicle was sandbagged to reduce the effects of blast; some of the vehicles were specially armoured; and roads were searched at first light each day. Still, as the Radfan campaign wore on, there was a steady toll of casualties from mines.

We were lucky. In the whole time I was in Aden not one of our unit vehicles went up on a mine. But luck it was: once, at Dhala, a whole company passed right over a mine, which blew up under an FRA vehicle just behind. Others were less lucky. Everyone learnt to live with the mines though – even the crews of the Ferrets, who ran the greatest risk, on the cheerful assumption that if a mine went off the chances were that it would be under someone else's vehicle; and if it was yours, you did not necessarily get hurt.

This, then, was one of the ways in which the dissidents hoped to wear down the British and the FRA, by killing men, or at least by tying down troops protecting the roads. It was ideal work for dissidents, as they could strike when and where they chose and could be far away before the mine exploded. They blew up a few vehicles and wounded a number of men. Mining was a nuisance, of a particularly unpleasant kind. It never became more serious than that.

The other popular dissident activity was shooting at the camps in the valley, in the late evening or at night, with rifle and light machine guns, and occasionally with rocket launchers, briefly and then disappearing. I never heard of anyone on our side being hurt from one of these attacks in the Radfan itself. There were a few near misses, but on the whole it was regarded as light entertainment or a tiresome interruption to the daily business.

The *Radfan Reader*, the local news-sheet, reproduced a marvellous eye-witness account from an Egyptian newspaper of one of these attacks. I forget the exact wording, but the general tone was *'...as the rocket launcher bombs burst in the camp tents burst into flames, and the British soldiers ran screaming for safety, with loud cries of 'farkin'. The laughing dissidents poured bullets into this scene of chaos. At least twenty British were killed and many more wounded...'*

This was funny, until we reflected that many Arab readers no doubt believed these stories, just as many Arabs no doubt believed the equally strange and fantastic stories broadcast. The Arabs were not fools, and those nearby had a truer picture. For many, though, the Arab broadcasts and such reports as this were the only news they had of the war in the Radfan. What was actually going on in the Radfan was no longer of primary importance. What mattered was the 'image' that was being created for the Arabs, both in the Federation and outside. Such stories as this were only a part of that image.

The valley of the Taim was a big area. Apart from the four main patrol bases, I had to guard the Rabwa Pass, put a picquet on Cap Badge and provide fifty men for local picquets around the Thumier base. With X Company still at Dhala and Support Company manning their mortars and machine guns again, I had few enough men to patrol an area of nearly forty square miles

I had to take the pressure off the rifle companies somehow. Before leaving Aden I had personally gone through the entire list of the unit and put a large cross against the name of every man I considered could be spared from administrative duties. These men, many of them drivers, took over the picquet duties at Thumier and at other places and took their turns at patrolling. They did their jobs very well, and virtually released the rifle companies for the main tasks and the main places.

The problem that had looked so easy from the mountain tops proved difficult. From the air or from our camps on the slightly higher ground the valley looked flat. When we got into the valley we found it intersected by dozens of small wadis. I went down the middle of the valley once by day with two Marines to look more closely at the ground we would have to patrol over. There was little chance of the dissidents being there by day, but we moved carefully, following the lines of small wadis cut into the surface of the valley, moving through patches of scrub and camel thorn, skirting the deserted villages. At times, where the wadis cut deep or there was thick scrub, we could see only twenty yards. This was by day, when there were no dissidents to find: it was confusing and close country

Houses in the Wadi Taim

I had known it by night too, from our 'night exercise' during our last stay in the valley. The Wadi Taim itself cut deep into the floor of the valley, in places twenty foot or more with sheer sides, where you might have to move a hundred yards to find a way across.

The relative flatness that had made it look so easy from the mountains made it easy for the dissidents too. In the mountains there were relatively few routes; and if we found a likely intersection and got there secretly, there was a reasonable chance that sooner or later some dissidents would pass by. Here the dissidents could move anywhere. We might have a hunch that the dissidents used a certain route, and we would ambush a particular spot. The dissidents might pass fifty yards away unseen in the darkness. We could string a line of twenty ambushes across the valley every night for a week: the dissidents might not come that way; or they might come into the valley from the sides – and even if they approached the line, there would be gaps of 300 yards between ambushes.

The problem was mathematical. We could increase the number of ambushes and cut down their size or vice versa. Always, though, the mathematics depended upon the pressure of work we could get out of the rifle companies and the number of men we could have without sleep each night. Once again the rifle companies were to be pushed to the limit.

They showed that their limit was high. At least their base camps were tolerably secure and comfortable and the food good, and they could rest well on their days off duty. They patrolled hard, and at times there were twenty-five patrols out in a single night. But the mathematics, with so few men, did not match the ground. We needed luck.

At first it looked as though we were going to get it.

The previous unit had concentrated on ambushing the tracks. I decided to try a different approach. I allotted Z Company the western end of the Taim – the Danaba Basin, Cap Badge and the Rabwa Pass. They were thin on the ground, but they could put ambushes of four men on the tracks each night.

HQ had Paddy's Field, with one troop attached – first Recce Troop, then a troop of Z Company. We put out four-man patrols on the nearby tracks and into the centre of the valley. Commando HQ took their share of patrols, the adjutant, signals officer and others taking their turn.

The main effort was to be at the eastern end of the valley, at 'Table Top' and Blair's Field, where at least we knew that the dissidents came each evening for a shooting match. Y Company were to bear the brunt of the work. At first they had both places; later, when X Company joined us, they were concentrated at Blair's Field, the most active spot, with Recce Troop to help them.

Z Company had a quiet month. They patrolled hard but never got a sight of a dissident, nor did the dissidents come near them. The Halmaini produced a kind of 'Home Guard', which provided extra patrols to the north, and Jungle Baizley's main entertainment was working with them. They used to come in every morning for briefing, a cheerful, colourful crowd. Each day the 'briefings' would get longer as tea and cigarettes were produced for them, and afterwards they would be 'drilled' by the CSM – a hilarious business: the Arab sense of humour proved to be remarkably like the English.

Twice joint patrols of Halmaini and Commandos went off to the north – tactically frightening, as the Halmaini quickly got bored with tactical movement if there was no shooting; and the return journey degenerated into a cavalcade with frequent halts for debate and shooting practice.

The Halmaini did not seem good in the dark, showing little sense in their choice of ambush positions. One night a shot passed over Monk's Field, the only shot Z Company had near them. I sent Z Company a signal of congratulations; but next morning the Halmaini said that it was one of their patrols reporting its position.

This kind of thing, and the interesting attempts to work camels for the re-supply of the picquets above the Rabwa Pass, was about all that Z Company had to break the monotony of a month's hard patrolling.

They had one moment of near tragedy, typical of the incidental difficulties of work in the Radfan. A young corporal, Bagshaw, a fine athlete and the Middle East Cross-country champion, had a picquet on a small sheer-sided hill south of the Rabwa Pass. One day the side of the cliff collapsed and he fell 100 feet on to a scree slope. One of the Marines, a cliff climber, got down to him and gave first aid, while the picquet sent a radio report. A Scout picked up Baizley and our doctor and a coil of rope and flew them to the picquet position – the Scout could not land on the scree slope. Baizley, an experienced cliff climber himself, roped the doctor down to Bagshaw. A Whirlwind with a winch was called up from Khormaksar, a special stretcher was lowered, and Bagshaw was hauled up and flown straight to hospital. Baizley hauled a rather white-faced doctor up the cliff again: new to Commandos, he had never been over a cliff before. Bagshaw was lucky, only a hairline fracture of the pelvis; and he was running again within a few months.

The further east one went the more active life became. From Paddy's Field, Recce Troop, with patrols of four men, made contacts on their first two nights, but both times fleeting and inconclusive – a shadow in the bottom of a wadi, which suddenly formed into three men who ran; and a group of four men who passed swiftly across a patch of moonlit sand at long range. It was disappointing; but it told us that there were dissidents to catch if only we had the judgement and the luck to put an ambush at the right place on the right night. We searched the valley by day, and found footprints and other traces, and slowly built up a pattern that suggested the kind of routes the dissidents might take. As the month went on and the state of the moon changed, so did the pattern of dissident movement.

The 'break' never came. Corporal French of the Recce Troop, who had spotted the shadows in the wadi bottom, went out on several nights, following a hunch about dissident routes. The dissidents came past one night just as the ambush was moving into position – they passed fifty yards away on a different route. The patrol fired quickly, but the dissidents disappeared into the night. There were more contacts, fleeting and inconclusive, though once a trace of blood was found next morning. As the month wore on the contacts in the middle of the valley ceased.

The dissidents came to us once at Paddy's Field, right at the beginning. The stillness of the night was broken by the shattering explosion of a rocket launcher bomb and a crackle of rifle fire, and then silence again. They had fired at one of our picquets 1,000 yards to the north, the bomb had passed harmlessly wide and landed half-way to Commando HQ (they were ever bad shots with the rocket launcher in the Wadi Taim), and the picquet and a nearby ambush opened fire. The picquet reported that they had seen and hit a dissident with tracer, but that he had got back out of sight. Next day we fixed up one of our own rocket launchers, on fixed lines and electrically detonated it, directed towards the most likely hill; but the dissidents never came to Paddy's Field again.

At 'Table Top' the story was much the same, though with added spice: the dissidents fired at it fairly regularly, from long range – just before dusk and very briefly, so that there was no chance of following up. We put ambushes out, but there was a lot of ground to cover. Four times the ambushes spotted dissidents, but always at long range. Once an ambush of six men spotted a group moving into a deserted village, and stalked them in the gathering dusk. They got into the village as the dissidents fired, but they were spotted, and the dissidents slipped out. Another small ambush on high ground on the south side of the wadi saw eight green-uniformed dissidents. They held their fire, but the dissidents went the wrong way. They then controlled mortar fire on to the dissidents, and the bombs fell accurately among them as the dissidents were getting ready to fire at 'Table Top'. They followed them with the mortar fire, trying to drive them to within shooting distance of the ambush, and gave the dissidents an unpleasant half-hour; but night came and the dissidents escaped.

The dissident's fire, always brief, was sometimes accurate, and once hit the casing of a Vickers gun – this was the third time that one of X Company's guns was hit. We could not ambush everywhere, so mortars and Vickers were laid on some areas so that fire could be brought down quickly and accurately. We even brought a Mobat up, to snipe back at the dissidents. It scored hits twice at places where the dissidents had fired from, and the firing stopped abruptly, but the morning patrols found nothing.

So it went on in its frustrating way, with two or three possibles but never that only guarantee of success, the body of a dead dissident. The only sign that we were having an effect was that the firing was less frequent, briefer and from longer range.

Blair's Field, at the eastern end of the valley, was the busiest place. The dissidents fired at it most evenings, as usual briefly, at long range and shortly before dusk. The firing, sometimes with a light machine gun, was occasionally accurate; but usually life went on much as usual, the resting men continuing to rest, the cooks continuing to cook. Once the visiting RC Chaplain – who fortunately had a sense of humour – was caught in the shower and had to jump for it as a burst of fire cut through the low scrub beside him.

The hard and dangerous business lay in the patrolling. The ground was rougher at this end of the valley, and Blair's Field was surrounded by low, broken hills about

800 yards away. Our predecessors had had no luck in their patrolling here, so we adopted the twenty-four and forty-eight hour ambushes as the most promising course. It wasn't easy. There were no villages here, and no scrub on the bare hilltops, and the small ambushes would have to lie up all day in the great heat, almost still, waiting for the evening performance. We put the ambushes out beyond the ring from which the dissidents shot, and hoped to catch them as they moved to or from their firing positions.

The first contact came on the second night, when a four-man patrol spotted a group of dissidents – at extreme range as ever – in the Wadi Taim itself, just west of Blair's Field. The patrol opened fire. Three of the dissidents escaped south, the fourth, believed hit, broke north. Another group of dissidents opened fire from nearby, and the company was quickly deployed from a series of ambushes on their escape route. As ever they disappeared. Possible traces of blood were found near where the dissident had been reported hit. No more.

Two nights later a patrol of six men, commanded by Lieutenant Bell, moving out to an ambush position to the north, heard voices and stopped. They could just see a group of four men in the moonlight, crossing an open space in front of them fifty yards away. They fired. Again the dissidents disappeared – more frustration.

They moved on, found their ambush position on a low hill among a tangle of intersecting wadis, and waited. They lay there all day in the hot sun, scarcely able to move, taking turns to scan the broken ground through binoculars.

In the late afternoon firing started from near Blair's Field, and soon afterwards the ambush saw four dissidents moving back quickly along the wadi, at long range, only the heads visible, and likely to pass well clear of the ambush. Bell took three men and cut across the wadis to intercept. The dissidents got past, but suddenly appeared in an open wadi 300 yards away, standing out now in their olive green uniforms and khaki turbans but moving fast. The ambush fired and missed, and the dissidents dived for cover. Bell called for artillery fire on his radio, and it came down right on target. One of the dissidents left his cover and ran, was hit almost simultaneously by two tracer bullets, and fell back and didn't move again. The others got into a small wadi and were heavily engaged with rifle and gunfire. Soon dust covered the valley, and nothing more was seen.

During the following weeks other ambushes fired, but always the contacts were fleeting, at long range and inconclusive. Twice dissidents were spotted moving into fire positions, mortar and artillery fire were brought down within seconds right on to them, and they disappeared. It was always near dusk, and the small ambush parties, sometimes only three men, could not safely go out to investigate the possible 'kills'.

I thought of pushing forward to find the dissident base. It could have been anywhere to our east near the Wadi Bana, and without definite intelligence it might take weeks to find. If we found it, or even moved forward to another line of hills three miles east of

Blair's Field, what then? There were more hills beyond, stretching far into the distance; the dissidents would find a new base, and we would be left with more of this dreary landscape to protect, which would have needed more men, or caused the present men to work even harder. This would have suited the dissidents well, extending us even further.

No, we would have to accept that the dissidents had the initiative. As long as they chose to strike at Blair's Field, where they were doing no harm at all and wasting a lot of time and energy, and giving us a chance to hit them when they came, that was fine by us.

Two miles north of Blair's Field a Wadi called Sha'ab Qatana ran parallel to the Wadi Taim and provided a likely route for dissidents between the Bana and the main alley of the Taim. The country there was particularly difficult, a tumbled mass of small ridges and hills up to 500 feet high, intersected by narrow wadis. I decided to ambush this. It was here that we had our first setback – an unpleasant reminder of the risks to both sides of patrolling in this kind of country.

Captain Goddard took the Recce Troop out in three mutually supporting patrols, two on hilltops, and the third in the bottom of the wadi below. The going was more difficult than had appeared from the air – it always was – and the third section was late getting into position. They took the risk of crossing a wadi just after first light, and waited. They had been seen. Three hours later there was a sudden burst of firing – two of the men had seen a dissident who had stumbled round a corner close by, had run out to grab him, and been shot down by another group of dissidents on higher ground, the corporal killed and the Marine wounded.

Goddard and his section above had not seen the dissidents moving in through the scrub in the narrow wadi, but they now went into action with rifles and LMGs. One of the dissidents was hit by a tracer bullet, and the light machine gun raked the ridge they were firing from. Another group of dissidents opened fire from further east, and they too were quickly engaged. The dissidents nearby made a short attempt to return fire; then, as ever, they disappeared.

The firing died down, the corporal's body and the wounded Marine were carried back to a safe place and flown out by Scout, and Recce Troop went back to their position and waited. We heard from the Halmaini some days later that a dissident had been killed and another wounded in the Sha'ab Qatana. The honours were probably even; but we didn't like it, and tried all the harder in our ambushes.

So it went on. The ambushes continued. Twice Godfrey Seager took out the whole company in a ring of ambushes, once round the Sha'ab Qatana and once in the hills east of Blair's Field. On the first one they shot at some dissidents at long range. On the second they opened fire at a group of dissidents, more dissidents joined in, and a firefight lasted for two hours. On another occasion an ambush party of four men on a hillside heard dissidents shooting at Blair's Field from around a corner only 100 yards away: as they set out to stalk them torrential rain came down and the dissidents vanished. There were 'possibles' reported on these and other contacts; but the luck never fell quite right, and we never achieved a close ambush or secured a body.

There were reports later of six dissidents killed at the eastern end of the Wadi Taim. These could have been, in part or all, from air strikes; or they could have been ours. The only sign that our patrolling was having an effect was the dissidents, who had been firing from quite close by when we arrived, now found 1,500 yards more expedient. But they still came.

It was a strange kind of fighting: the dissidents firing at Blair's Field most afternoons, pointlessly and ineffectively, hardly disturbing the routine of the camp: the ambushes out on their hot hilltops all day, hoping that sooner or later mathematics and chance would bring a dissident into their sights. It was tiring work and boring work, for a man must be alert all the time – might never see a dissident the whole time he was in the Radfan, yet must be ready for those few seconds when he might see or be seen.

The Marines took it phlegmatically, sometimes enthusiastically, though the enthusiasm fell off as tiredness and boredom came after days of fruitless patrolling. The politics of it puzzled them a little, that we should be keeping Arabs out of Arab land; but they accepted the reasons and went about their business efficiently.

I don't believe there was ever any venom during the whole time in the Radfan. I saw two poems written by men of the unit – not particularly good poems, except for their content, which showed a quiet awareness that there were real men at the other end of the valley, with problems much the same as their own. The more sympathetic of these poems was written by a young corporal who patrolled harder than anyone. They thought about it: that done, they went about their business.

The routine went on throughout the valley, sometimes increasing, sometimes falling off so that men could be rested. There was neither success nor failure, just the routine, keeping the tribes out until they came to terms. No great victories to be won, nor big defeats to be suffered; a great deal of risk, and tiredness, at both ends of the valley.

Sometimes rumours drifted through the market places around the Radfan. The dissidents were having their troubles. There were reports of casualties, of defections, of quarrels, of a convoy of arms snaffled by a neutral tribe because the dissidents had not paid their toll money; of dissatisfaction because too much of the promised pay stuck to the fingers of chiefs and lieutenants; of resistance by the tribes to the discipline the hard core dissidents tried to impose.

There were stories, too, of new weapons and large convoys of arms and ammunition arriving in the Radfan, and of great new concentrations of dissidents in the Wadi Bana, many hundreds. Nothing ever came of these large concentrations, and we learnt to accept them as part of the Arab world, where stories were passed through places, each teller adding his own dramatic flourish. Within them somewhere were pieces of truth, usually too deep for the inexperienced to perceive them. The stories told us only that the men at the end of the valley were having their casualties and their problems, just as we were.

This phase of the Radfan campaign was nearly over. The tribes had had enough, and nearly all of them had offered arms and hostages as guarantees of their future behaviour. Some of the tribes were already back and working in their fields.

For us the pattern of the operation so far had been simple. The dissidents and the tribes had been defeated in battle and driven out of the Radfan; thereafter the dissidents had been kept out, their activities confined largely to the eastern end of the Wadi Taim, where they did little harm. True, some British and FRA soldiers had been killed and wounded, and the rest had had to work very hard, and were tired. But the limited tasks we had been given had been achieved.

These were the facts. But military facts are only a small part of the content of such indecisive campaigns. Who knows what great victories had been won in the Radfan on the radio and on paper and in the market places? The picture presented would have been unrecognisable to us, just as the account of the attack on the British camp was unrecognisable. The picture no doubt had its effect in some places. Yet the effect was less than it might have been. The other tribes in the Federation showed little sympathy for the dissidents, and the attempts to create trouble elsewhere were held in check, without too much difficulty, by the FRA and the FNG.

In late September we returned to Little Aden, and that was the last I saw of the Radfan. It had been a fascinating month in its way, not as easy as we had expected – we should have learnt by then that the Radfan never was. The dissidents were as elusive as ever, flitting through the wadis and low hills. Yet we had made contact many times, usually on our own terms, and this alone was an achievement and a deterrent for the dissidents. During the long period of patrolling that began in June we had killed or wounded more dissidents than all the other units in the Radfan, even if our 'possibles' were not included.

I was frustrated when I got back to Little Aden, frustrated and tired. There was no physical reason for this tiredness; in the later days in the Radfan I had less to do than anyone in the Commando. There had been the daily visits to the camps or the outlying posts, discussions on the patrolling plan, the evening conferences at HQ; in between, almost nothing, the heat discouraging the routine of office work during the day, and at night hot and stuffy inside a blacked-out tent. I was frustrated because there was little I could do personally. The work lay with the company commanders and below – with the patrol commanders, and with the Marines, on patrol every other night and on night guards between patrols. The ultimate responsibility, though, lay with me, and I felt it, as I had not done throughout the year.

During the year we had made mistakes. In September we had a run of mistakes, most of them small, one or two serious. I felt that because of the pressure of events, the heavy commitments in Aden even more than in the Radfan, we were becoming ‘accident prone’. The heat did not help me to see it all objectively.

By the eternal process all the trivial injustices, real or imagined, of the past year came to mind, and by the same process the frustration was transposed into righteous indignation. I was about to transpose it further into some kind of action – I never discovered what – when a senior staff officer, a very busy man, came out from Aden on a casual visit. I let my hair down. That, I don’t doubt, was what he came for. At the end he laughed and said he had commanded a unit three times and it hadn’t changed at all.

That evening we had a small party on the patio outside the mess. It was pleasant there, surrounded by the flowers and trees and exotic shrubs of the garden first planted there by the officers of 45 Commando four years before, drinking under the stars with the strange red glow of the flame from the BP pylon flickering over the trees. Significantly, the wind had shifted a little, and was cooler on the cheek, and the flame was blowing out further. It was the end of a long summer.

Chapter 13

The Dhala Road

Within a few days, as the cool season came on us, spirits lightened, tempers settled and energy returned as it had done a year before. My gloom of the previous week seemed ridiculous as a sense of proportion returned. There had been no great battles, no great risks for many months, no real strain, only the monotony of the work in the Radfan and in Aden and the greater monotony of the heat. The work remained as hard as ever, but with the coming of the cool season we took it more easily.

Our work in the Radfan had been, indirectly, keeping the Dhala Road open. When we left the Radfan in September it was not for a rest but for a change, to operate at the two ends of the Dhala Road.

At the northern end, near the Yemen border, at Dhala itself, paradise had lost some of its attractions. Early in the year the dissidents had begun mining and sniping there; and when the Radfani not only failed to stop the traffic on the road but lost the dissidents' face as well, the dissidents stepped up their activities in Dhala.

They began with attacks on isolated posts of the Federal National Guard, and by June were shooting by night at the FRA and Royal Marines camps, with rifles and light machine guns, later with rocket launchers, later still with 81mm mortars – no joke in these crowded camps on small flat hills. The fire was usually inaccurate but it took some of the pleasure out of Dhala. X Company, who had worked hard in the Radfan, were sour when they found, on arriving at the 'rest camp', that the pressure of work was at least as high as in the Radfan.

The FRA and the Commando company soon adjusted themselves to the new life, of training and resting by day and patrolling and 'standing to' at night. After a while the nightly firework display was treated on its merits, and men not on duty slept through it, ignoring the occasional shots over the camp and the sudden bursts of fire from our own support weapons. There were narrow escapes. One Marine returned from night guard to find a bullet in his pillow. An officer was temporarily deafened by a rocket launcher bomb exploding a few yards from him – one of the few that actually landed in the camp.

On the whole the business there was regarded as dull. Ambushes were put out every night, and mortar and Vickers fire was put down quickly on the dissidents who fired. One dissident was shot and later reported to have died. Another group, firing from a nearby hill, were hit directly by mortar and Vickers fire, and bloodstains were found later beside their empty cartridge cases.

Part of the twisting and dangerous single-track Dhala Road near Khuraibah Pass

When the unit left the Radfan in September it was Y Company's turn to go to Dhala. They had a four day rest at Little Aden; most of it spent on the beach, then went to Dhala and tackled the problems there with remarkable relish. Godfrey Seager re-organised the defences, built even higher sandbag walls so that men off duty could sleep peacefully, put a Mobat on top of Temple Hill – a high hill 400 yards north of the camp – to deal with snipers, and established a high tempo of patrolling.

The luck never ran their way on patrols, and they had no contacts. Then, one night in late October, a group of dissidents came too close to the camp and one was shot – a solitary success from weeks of hard patrolling and night guards.

The atmosphere in the camp was anything but tense. One night two young Marines, reinforcements fresh from England, turned up nicely dressed at the Transport tent – marked 'Dhala Taxis' – and asked for a taxi to take them to the night club in Dhala town, which their chums had strongly recommended. There was much arranging of cars and escorts and fatherly advice from the guard, interrupted only when the Duty Sergeant heard of it and sent the men back to their tents, on the grounds that they were not wearing ties.

At the end of October Godfrey Seager celebrated the 300th Anniversary of the Royal Marines with a fadhal – meal in Arab style – for the Emir of Dhala and the officers of the FRA, and with demonstrations of firepower for the inhabitants of the valley. The demonstration, as well staged as if it had been at a school in England, ended with the ceremonious firing of a new and secret kind of mortar bomb, brightly painted, which exploded at the far end of the valley with a great mushroom cloud. Curiously, the Commando camp was left unmolested for nearly a fortnight after that.

In early November Y Company came down to Little Aden. The whole unit was to be concentrated there for two months, for rest and re-training, and Dhala Camp was left without a Commando garrison for the first time for four years. Y Company were sorry to leave, even sorrier to return to the hot and crowded camp at Little Aden. Dhala had been pleasant: the work was hard, but it was real work; the frequent shooting by the dissidents was little more than a nuisance; and the only real frustration was the inability to catch the dissidents. Even the drivers, who, with the constant threat of mines under the rough tracks, might have been expected to dislike it most, were sorry to leave. At Dhala they had their own trucks and their own jobs to do, and they escaped the absolute paternal care of the Transport Officer.

At the other end of the Dhala Road the rest of the unit had been busy, in Aden itself. The dissidents had been busy there too. So far their bomb and rocket attacks in and near the town had been largely incompetent and ineffective, but there were signs of more trouble. Within twenty-four hours of our return from the Radfan the unit had gone on to Internal Security duties, guarding key points, patrolling and standing by in the town for trouble. With only two rifle companies, the pressure was as high as in the Radfan, and much less pleasant.

I doubt if any troops enjoy Internal Security work of this kind, waiting night after night, guarding dreary places, the initiative always with the other side, able to strike when and where they chose. Even when called out to deal with a riot – and this never happened to us in 1964 – there is more waiting, perhaps standing motionless under a shower of stones and garbage, or the imminent prospect of that. The troops are seldom required to act. Their very presence, on guard or before a patrol or before a mob, is usually enough, provided they look the part. But the troops cannot be everywhere, and with all key points guarded the dissidents turn to the easy targets – civilians, even women and children, soon to become the target in Aden.

The elections for Aden State were due on 16 October. By the time we had got down from the Radfan there had already been incidents – a rocket launcher fired at Khormaksar airfield and several bombings. The National Front for the Liberation of the Occupied Yemen South had promised to wreck the elections, and had warned all electors to boycott the elections.

We revised our Internal Security drills – the formations and movements for clearing streets, for breaking up mobs, for using tear gas, for establishing road blocks and so on. It was dull work, the more so coming between nights on guard or on patrol. We livened it up by making the companies take turn and turn about as riot squads and mobs, and noted their preference for the latter. John Lloyd and Support Company provided a very efficient and correct mob for Baizley and Z Company, withering away in the face of the imaginary tear gas. When Baizley's turn came as mob leader Z Company played every dirty trick in the book including lynching two of Support Company. John said Z Company hadn't played fair, Baizley said mobs didn't play fair anyway, and the acrimonious argument was only ended by my ordering a replay next day.

This was all useful stuff, and the companies' reaction time speeded up a lot both against fair and unfair tactics. Nevertheless one cynical captain pointed out that the companies still showed greater enthusiasm and skill as mobs than as riot squads, and that a bystander ignorant of the effect of tear gas might draw the wrong conclusions. He also pointed out that there were bystanders, and that reports would no doubt filter back to places in Aden, where people might draw the wrong conclusions. His cynical mind produced a remedy. Thereafter every exercise ended with crashing volleys and groaning bodies. This may have damaged our image, but we liked to think that it had the proper effect.

As the elections approached there were more incidents and the unit was deployed. We remained throughout the day and night of the election, in reserve in central places and with patrols near likely trouble spots. Other troops were out too, all striking a careful balance between political discretion and a show of readiness. The elections passed quietly, with a very high percentage of the electorate voting.

In mid November we came off Internal Security, and a few days later Y Company joined us. For the first time for nearly a year we had nothing to do but train and enjoy ourselves. We worked hard, but we played hard too, and with success. The soccer team was top of the league, unbeaten except when they took on the Combined Services; the rugger team was unbeaten, with only six points scored against it; the cross-country team swept the board, and in one match open to all three Services produced eight out of the first twelve home. Only a fortnight after our return from the Radfan we produced all but three of the Royal Naval swimming team, which came a close second in the Inter-Services match.

Every unit had its successes, and selects and arranges them to look nice. These were ours, and to us we looked very beautiful indeed. It may all have been irrelevant to our duties and our efficiency, but after a hard year it was satisfying, as we relaxed, to feel that we were not losing our touch.

We remembered that this was the Tercentenary Year of the Royal Marines, meriting some pageantry or ceremony. We dusted off the plans we had made earlier in the year, but found them impracticable. They required time for preparation, and all the time we had got we needed for training, as we might be called to the Radfan or elsewhere any day. We compromised by entertaining all our friends in Aden one evening, and a few days later we entertained ourselves, with camel races, side shows and a concert.

A BBC broadcast to mark the Tercentenary included a recording by CSM Abraham of Y Company, twenty-five years with the Corps and a Commando of World War II. He said:

> *A young Marine of today is better material than ever before. You can't put it down to one thing. He's getting a better education. His upbringing at home, which is always maligned a great deal, seems to be a better upbringing. Whether it's the better standard of living or what it is I wouldn't know, but he's a better turned out chap than when I was young. No matter what you throw at them they seem to take it in their stride. The enthusiasm is always there, even on menial tasks. They don't require whipping along, they're always eager to get on with the job and get it finished. They ask more questions, because they want to know, they're interested. No matter what the conditions are they seem undisturbed, enthusiastic, and they get on with the job.*

I have hardly mentioned individual Marines in this book. I have taken them for granted, as I did at the time. They only needed to be told what to do and they did it as best they could, which was usually very well indeed. Some of them were very young. It is the common practice to be rude about the youth of today – it has always been so, but seems more so today. Perhaps it is because they are more dynamic and more vocal, so that the worst of them are prominent and tiresome, and the best tiresome too, because they ask difficult questions. Maligning the young is the most ancient of customs. It is a pity, at such a time as this, that we are not more aware of the potential that lies around us.

My own time in the unit was nearly up, and there was much to do after a hectic year to put the administration tidy for my successor. Commando HQ worked hard to prepare the supersession musters. Skeletons were found, and either sorted and labelled or decently buried. There were shocks: I found, in my house, an electricity bill for £10,000; which, even with my air-conditioner on at night, seemed steep. It was found to refer to the whole of Little Aden, and I passed it on.

I flew up the Dhala Road for the last time. Thumier, which I had first known as a small and bare airstrip with a few tents round it, was now a great complex of tracks and huts and tented camps around a large and busy airfield. I could see clearly the route we had taken on our first night march to 'Coca Cola': it had long since been made into a road, and it looked easy. Beyond was Cap Badge, seeming small from the air, but still the key to the Wadi Taim. To the south were the high mountains: I had first known them as a vague, forbidding mass: now I could put a name to every peak. Below us was the thin ribbon of the Dhala Road with the occasional dust clouds from convoys or Arab trucks. At the end of the road was Dhala, looking green and peaceful.

There were a lot of memories, pleasant and unpleasant.

Aden had changed a lot since our first light-hearted exercise in the desert. I had enjoyed it, each phase in the changing pattern, perhaps more in retrospect than at the time. One thing was certain. I was bored with the Radfan.

I paid my last visits in Aden. I was dined out by the officers, and I spoke to the unit, the last of many times. On 20 November my successor (Lieutenant Colonel Robin McGarel-Groves) arrived, bursting with enthusiasm. On 22 November I left him on his own at Khormaksar airfield and caught the night charter flight to England. The aircraft was, as ever, full of squalling children; but I slept well, ignoring the twinges of memory of things left undone or partly done. They were no longer my business.

High over England the sun was shining coldly, a different sun from the one that had seemed a permanent part of my life for so long. It disappeared as we descended through thick cloud over Gatwick. That was the last I saw of it for five days, but it was nice to be back in England.

WANTED!!!
DEAD OR ALIVE
RADFAN PADDY!

THE COMMANDANT GENERAL

OFFERS :-

£100 REWARD

FOR INFORMATION LEADING TO THE CAPTURE OF THE ABOVE UNSHAVEN, UNWASHED, DISHEVELLED, MALODOROUS DESPERADO MASQUERADING AS A COLONEL OF HER MAJESTY'S ROYAL MARINES.

AS CAN BE SEEN— THIS MAN IS MEAN & HIGHLY DANGEROUS BUT IS EASILY HUMOURED BY OFFERING HIM A ROTHMANS KING SIZE